STONE
WALLS

STONE WALLS

Prisons from Fetters to Furloughs

By

MIRIAM ALLEN DeFORD

CHILTON BOOKS

A Division of Chilton Company
Publishers
Philadelphia and New York

To VALVERDA M. BOOTH

For Many Reasons,
Some of Which She Knows

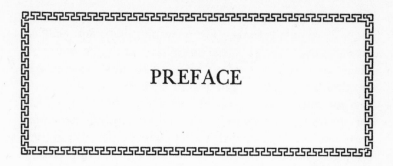

PREFACE

The easiest way to explain what a book is about is to tell what it is *not* about.

This is a history of prisons and prison systems, all over the civilized world, from the earliest beginnings to today and beyond that to tomorrow. To say it formally, it is a history of penology, with special reference to the evolution of prison reform from its first effective start in the eighteenth century, to its contemporary status, with some extrapolation of its probable future progress—perhaps to the day when prisons, as such, will be as extinct as slave galleys are today.

It is neither a history of criminology nor of confinement of a "non-criminal" nature (e.g., confinement in mental institutions or poorhouses); nor is it a history of capital punishment or any other form of punishment for law-breaking except by institutionalization. Some of these will be touched upon, incidentally, as part of the continuing narrative of what men do to their fellow beings who offend against the social rules of their time and place.

It does not cover prisoners-of-war or concentration camps, as distinguished from prison camps in time of peace, for those confined in them are not criminals in any genuine sense of the word. For the same reason, it does not cover political prisoners as such, except insofar as they are imprisoned together with criminal offenders in already established institutions. (For example, the infamous Nazi concentration camps were organized and run solely as places in which to shut up—or destroy—men, women and children whose only crime was to have the "wrong" ethnic descent. Such actual criminals as were posted in them were for the most part members of the controlling personnel and were being rewarded, rather than punished, for their offenses against civil law. On the other hand, the Russian penal labor camps, though to some extent they were—perhaps still are—places of "punishment" for those with the "wrong" political or economic convictions, were also lineal descendants of the penal colonies of Czarist days and hence have always included a number of "ordinary" prisoners, thus coming within the scope of this book. As a final example, the iniquitous camps or colonies in which, during World War II, our own country confined those of Japanese birth or descent who had the misfortune to live in the Pacific Coast states, are as much outside the purpose of the book as would be the Roman mines in which captured enemies slaved till they died, or the internment points which all nations established to hold captured officers and men of the enemy forces.) Prison is an institution to which people are sentenced after conviction of crime.

Though there are many weighty volumes (the more important of which are listed in the bibliography) which treat exhaustively of the main subject of this volume, there is no brief, up-to-date book in English which treats exclusively of prisons and their gradual reform from their dreadful beginnings. Indeed, it is a subject which many persons interested in social reform actually fail to consider. For example, as recently as 1960, a 600-page book on late Victorian reformers completely omitted mention of one single prison reformer—though this was the period when, as we shall see, enormous steps were being taken to supplement the first early Victorian attempts at improvement in the treatment of prisoners.

Such tangential questions as probation, parole, the status of discharged prisoners and ex-convicts, and the problems of prisoners' families are of course an inherent part of any discussion of prison reform. But so far as possible this book limits itself to the actual condition of prisons and of their convicted inmates, as it was, as it is, and as it may be. These supplementary matters are covered only as illustration of and commentary on the main theme. As for the procedure which sends the inmate to the prison in the first place—his arrest, investigation, trial and verdict, his sentence and its possible appeals—these all belong in books on criminology, not in those on penology per se. We shall start here with the convicted and incarcerated prisoner and leave him at the prison gates with his discharge or release on parole. Sometimes we may seem to range beyond this limit, but only by way of relation to the prison itself.

Though so far as material is available we shall be describing and evaluating prisons and prison systems all over the civilized world, the chief emphasis is necessarily on those of the United States of America and Great Britain (and to a lesser extent those of Western Europe in general). Partly, this is because information in these areas is much more accessible than elsewhere (for instance, the newly formed nations of Africa and Asia are often far too busy with forming settled governments to have had time as yet to do much about such specific problems as those of prison reform); partly it is because to readers of English their own systems are naturally of the greatest interest; but very largely it is because it was actually in North America and England that prison reform began. The United States and the United Kingdom, despite great names and important movements in Western and Central

Europe, were the pioneers, interacting on each other, sometimes one, sometimes the other, being in the forefront. It was they who most influenced penologists in other lands, first on the Continent, then throughout the world.

However, if any nation on earth which today has prisons as punishment for lawbreakers and a developed penal system is omitted from mention in this book, it is only because it has been impossible to secure information. Either such a country is outside the international association now affiliated with the United Nations, or, as already said, it is still too recently organized to have as yet codified and published any account of its penal system. Perhaps, in the case of several still struggling with internal dissension or even with civil war, there is not yet anything pertinent to report.

I am well aware that for these reasons there are gaps and inadequacies in this book; there may be inaccuracies as well, though I have made use of all the information available to me. Sometimes this information, though true when it was written, may no longer be so. Covering the entire globe as this history does, I have not been able to visit most of the institutions of which I treat, but I have relied on firsthand reports when they were obtainable, and when they were not, on the statements of recognized experts in the field. What errors I may have committed are, I trust, negligible. I have tried conscientiously to cover up neither good nor bad wherever I found them. The only claim I make is that the over-all study presents a true general picture of the world's penal systems and a history in brief of the efforts made by devoted men and women to redeem their evils and to bring them into consonance with the advance of civilization.

With these reservations and exceptions, then, let us discover how prisons began, what social philosophy lay behind them, what they used to be like, what they are like now after at least two centuries of reform, and what their future may be. We are dealing here with men and women, boys and girls, often with mere children. Before they became felons or misdemeanants they were human beings like ourselves, and they remain our fellow humans, with all their potentialities for evil and for good, even when we have changed their names to numbers and locked them away from the society they have offended. That is the very heart of the social approach to prison reform.

MIRIAM ALLEN deFORD

ACKNOWLEDGMENTS

Grateful acknowledgment is made to the following publishers for permission to quote from the books named:

George Allen and Unwin, Ltd., London, for *The Dilemma of Penal Reform*, by Hermann Mannheim, copyright 1957.

The Bodley Head, Ltd., London, for *Prisons and Changing Civilization*, by M. Hamblin-Smith, copyright (by John Lane) 1934.

The Clarendon Press, Oxford, and Oxford University Press, New York, for *Penal Reform*, by Max Grünhut, copyright 1948.

Columbia University Press, New York, for *Punishment and Social Structure*, by Otto Kirchheimer and Georg Rusche, copyright 1939.

Thomas Y. Crowell Company, New York, for *Punishment and Reform*, by Frederick H. Wines, copyright 1923.

Doubleday & Company, Inc., New York, for *Flag on Devil's Island*, by Francis Lagrange (with William Murray), copyright 1961.

Doubleday & Company, Inc., New York, and Hutchinson and Company, Ltd., London, for *The House at Old Vine*, by Norah Lofts, copyright 1961.

CONTENTS

STONE WALLS

Section 1

YESTERDAY'S PRISONS

1

Prisons, in the sense in which we understand them, as places to which convicted criminals are sent for varying terms in punishment for their crimes, scarcely existed before the eighteenth century.

There were plenty of prisons, of course, from the earliest times of which we have historical record, but they were places of detention rather than places of incarceration. People were kept in them either until they were tried and sentenced or until they were executed or received other forms of corporal punishment—also, if they had not paid their fine, which was the actual punishment. As Ulpian, the Roman jurist, said in the third century, A.D., *"Carcer ad continiendos homines, non ad puniendos, haberi debet"* ("A prison ought to be maintained for holding men, not for punishing them"). In fact, according to Justinian's *Digest,* imprisonment in our meaning of the term was illegal by the Roman code.

This was decidedly not a gesture of mercy, or evidence of sympathy for the criminal, nor was there any idea of rehabilitating him. Until about two hundred years ago, such sentiments were practically unknown; criminals, like slaves captured in war, were pariahs. If they could be made

1

economically useful and their crimes were not too heinous to let them live, they could be worked to death in mines or quarries; otherwise the quickest and most economical way to dispose of them was to kill them. Lesser offenders were mutilated—hands, ears, or tongues cut out—branded, flogged, tortured in various ways, as a supposed deterrent or to make it physically impossible for them to repeat their crimes. This corporal punishment was a direct penalty for their crimes and was strictly differentiated from torture to secure confession, as, for example, in the Spanish Inquisition. (There is a contemporary vestige of this latter procedure in the police third degree.)

Lesser offenders suffered public shaming. They were put in the stocks or the pillory (sometimes they died there —accidentally—as a result of the stoning they might receive from the angry citizens who gathered to pelt them with garbage and to strike and spit on them). Women, whether scolds or suspected witches, petty criminals, or just plain malicious gossips, might be ducked or made to wear the brank or dame's bridle—an iron cagelike affair placed on the head, with a spike in the mouth to pierce a moving tongue. Sometimes prisoners were flogged or branded while they were in the pillory or stocks. (In both cases the hands and feet were locked in a frame. In the pillory the victim stood, while in the stocks he sat down.) Sometimes the victim's ears were nailed to the beams of the pillory; when he was released he had the choice of having them torn off roughly from the nails by the officer in charge or of tearing them out himself.

Mutilation was frequent, all the way from the Sumerian codes of Lipit-Ishtar and Eshnunna, about 1880 B.C. (the earliest we have, about a thousand years before Hammurabi's code and two thousand years before the Mosaic laws) until practically the present time in a few backward lands.

As for branding, that was not abolished in England un-

2

til 1829. Usually an offender was branded with a letter indicating his crime. The Romans branded on the forehead, and so have most governments since—but what later became the State of New Jersey used strict logic in the seventeenth century; burglars were branded with a "T" (for "thief") on the hand for their first offense, on the forehead with an "R" (for "robber") for the second.

Some of these brandings and mutilations were, as I have said, thought of as deterrents: thus a thief or a counterfeiter might have his hands cut off, a perjurer have his tongue cut out, a convicted spy have his eyes gouged from their sockets, or a rapist be castrated—thereby in every case effectively preventing his becoming a recidivist. But by some codes (e.g., mediaeval Denmark) dreadful mutilations were inflicted to make of the victim a mockery of humanity whom all would shun at sight—noseless, earless, or scalped.

Flogging was considered a light punishment or a mere subsidiary part of the punishment—after all, slaves, soldiers, sailors, and children were frequently flogged, though not with knotted ropes and not so thoroughly. Prisoners might be flogged "at the cart's tail"—i.e., tied to the back of a slowly moving cart that traveled the length of the town for a specified time, and followed by an officer armed with a whip who belabored the bare back of the man or woman undergoing the punishment. Oddly enough, there was relatively little flogging as a penalty in England until the twelfth century, except for offenses against the church; later it became a common punishment, and women were flogged publicly in England as late as 1817. We in America have no cause for smugness. Maryland did not repeal flogging until 1936, and it is still legal in Delaware, though more or less of a dead letter. England has now abolished flogging and other corporal punishment in prisons, but there is strong agitation in Parliament for its restoration.

3

I have mentioned fines as among the penalties substituted for imprisonment in early times. But at first fining was considered more like the payment of a debt. The very word "fine" comes from the Latin *finem facere* (to make an end): the debtor was held in custody until he (or more likely his relatives or friends) could pay; then his incarceration ended. It was closer to ransom than to punitive action. In mediaeval Germany, fines were divided into *bot* and *wite;* the *bot* was paid to the injured person or his representative to make peace with him for the injury, the *wite* was paid to the ruler whose peace had been disturbed. By the twelfth century, damages were assessed by a tribunal, taking the place of *bot*. *Wite* (which might previously have been substituted for by some other form of punishment) was transmuted into a monetary penalty. This is the essence also of the Anglo-Saxon *wergild*, and of all other systems of fines (dating back to the Sumerian code) which were thought of as compensation and carefully graded according to the rank, age, and sex of the injured person.

It is only a step from this to imprisonment for debt, which was universal until quite recent times and indeed still exists in such forms as imprisonment for failure to pay income tax or alimony. There is an echo of it in all penalties for misdemeanors, and even for some felonies, where the stated punishment is, say, a $500 fine or six months in jail, or both. A large proportion of the population of all jails is made up of inmates who were unable to pay the fine which was the alternative to incarceration.

In other words, our whole philosophy of punishment for crime has undergone a gradual evolution. To primitive peoples, any offense against the mores of the tribe can be due only to possession by evil spirits. The offender is punished—usually killed. He is a victim of the gods as much as if he were maimed or diseased, and his punish-

4

ment is a gesture to placate the powers that have brought evil on the people. Crime and sin are identical to the primitive, both are evidence of the anger of the gods; both, primarily, are a breaking of taboos.

In a little later stage, with the rise of kingship, crime becomes considered a willful offense against the social body. Man has free will, and if perversely he chooses to do wrong, he must suffer for it. But basically, private wrongs that do not affect society are the business of the wronger and the wronged. If the relatives of a murdered man do not seek their own revenge, nobody else will do it for them, and the murder may go entirely unpunished. Of course they nearly always did seek revenge; hence the long history of blood feuds, surviving into our own day.

Finally came the concept of compensation, with its elaborate lists of fines for every imaginable offense, victim, and perpetrator. Yet, the revenge motive persisted, and it still persists. It lies behind today's proponents of capital punishment and of "strict" prison conditions. It wants to see the criminal *punished,* not reformed.

Still, through all this evolution, simple imprisonment was hardly thought of as a penalty for crime. There are some exceptions: Plato, for example, was in favor of three grades of prisons—one a place of detention for those under arrest and not yet tried, one for minor offenders, and one for major criminals. There are prisoners in the Bible —Joseph after he repelled the advances of Potiphar's wife, Samson, and Jeremiah (though the last two might well be thought of as political prisoners).

According to canon law, in the late thirteenth century, members of the clergy who committed crimes could be imprisoned for life, or for a term sufficient to bring about their repentance. (And this despite the fact that for lay criminals the church was a place of sanctuary from which they could not be taken.) The Spanish Inquisition, indeed, recognized three types of prison: a public prison for offenders who had committed ordinary crimes, not "against the faith"; a prison for the disciplining of employees of the Holy Office itself, who had broken laws but were not accused of heresy; and, finally, the underground dungeons in which heretics were either buried forever, or kept until they confessed or succumbed under torture, or were handed over to "the secular arm" to be burned at the stake. (Napoleon broke into these dungeons in 1804, freed the wretched prisoners in them, and had the whole structure blown up.)

There were also some nonclerical anticipations of imprisonment as a form of punishment for crime. In England in 1275, men convicted of rape could be imprisoned for two years. In 1576, in the reign of Elizabeth I, men saved from hanging by pleading benefit of clergy (i.e., ability to read and write) could be thrown into the Tower of London for a year. In Germany, in 1530, one could get two weeks for blasphemy. And two years later, Emperor Charles V ordered imprisonment as a penalty for crime for petty thieves caught in the act. In fact, he almost anticipated the indeterminate sentence, by a provision under which convicted criminals who gave reason to expect that they would continue their criminal careers might be imprisoned until somebody had paid sufficient security to indemnify future victims.

But still these remained exceptions. Imprisonment as we know it, is a penalty for lawbreaking. It is a child of the industrial revolution. As Hans vonHentig put it, "Imprisonment grew from the pit, the stake, the cage, the fetter." Men were kept in prison only if and when "the advantages of letting a person live made up for the inconvenience of shutting him up, feeding and guarding him." To quote Otto Kirchheimer and Georg Rusche,

"Prisons were co-eval with the rise of industrialism. . . . Prisons came with the rise of mercantilism."

That this is so is evidenced by the fact that from the beginning it was the poor who were sent to prison. As Anatole France once observed, the law in its infinite justice forbids both the rich and the poor to sleep under bridges—but the rich don't have to. When stealing a pocket handkerchief could mean the gallows or transportation for an eight-year-old boy, there was no attempt to deny that it was the "lower classes" who were expected to fill the prisons. It was carefully made clear that under no conditions were prisons ever to offer a standard of living higher than that of the very poorest free subjects. (When a man of means did for some reason have to undergo a term of imprisonment, he could live in comfort or even in luxury out of his own pocket.) The justification, if any were needed, lay in the realization that the poor lived in such hardship and privation that a decent standard of living in prison would have been an incentive to, instead of a deterrent from, crime.

When there is a large surplus of cheap labor, including slave labor, it is cheaper to kill an offender than to support him in prison. But when, as in the rise of the industrial system at the end of the eighteenth century, labor is in demand, then it is advantageous to put the prisoner to work, free. That was not, decidedly, the mainspring of the early reformers, but even John Howard recognized the economic factor and advocated the use of prison labor. There were, of course, noneconomic factors as well: Spengler suggested one curious one, that with industrialism man became more time-conscious, and hence could contemplate the taking away of so many years of a man's life as a valid punishment for his offense against society. It is no accident that imprisonment as punishment became the most

7

frequent penal method from the latter part of the eighteenth century on.

2

What were prisons like before anyone thought of improving them?

First of all there was the slave kennel. A man could be enslaved as punishment for a crime in some times and places, though usually the slaves not born in servitude were captives or debtors. In the ruins of Pompeii, two skeletons were found shackled by their wrists to a wall in a room of the gladiators' quarters. Here again, it was a question of war prisoners, debtors, or slaves (and an occasional adventurous, aberrant, young freeman). Though a slave who committed a crime could be sold by his master to the gladiatorial school, all this ghastly find proves is that the gladiatorial school did have a room which served as a prison. Stocks were found there too.

When the Roman colony of Alba (founded in the fifth century B.C.) was excavated by archaeologists, subterranean chambers were found under the marketplace, which could be entered only from above. It is likely that these were dungeons. The Carthaginians dug galleries from the beach to limestone cliffs to serve as sandstone quarries; they were worked by prisoners who never left them alive, but wore out their wretched lives in them. But these, too, from all evidence, were prisoners of war or slaves, and there is no mention of the dungeons' being used for felons. It has even been suggested that the famous Cretan labyrinth was really a prison.

The Romans did have prisons, however. They used their earliest colonies (*vide* Alba's oubliettes) as detention points—though usually for prisoners of war—and in Rome itself there was the Mamertine Prison, with the dungeon, called the Tulliana, built under it later.

In England, as in most other places, the first prisons were, so to speak, privately owned. The king had prisons, usually dungeons, in his castles, but noblemen and bishops also had their own private prisons as part of their castles, fortresses, or mansions. They dispensed justice privately, and they could do as they liked with those they condemned. That is undoubtedly why both the English and the Continental nations were so slow to acknowledge that even a prisoner had to breathe and eat. As late as 1635, in Leipsic, a proto-reformer recommended that prisons should be "places where people could live, and have air and light"—a sufficient commentary on the lack of air and light in the prisons then existing.

The Tower of London, built by William the Conqueror in the eleventh century, was originally an arsenal. So, for example, was the Salpêtrière in Paris (then it was a beggars' hostel, then a prison for women, finally a general prison); most of the French prisons were originally constructed for other uses. The Bastille was one of the city gates, the Porte St. Antoine. In 1370 it was replaced by a fortress, but in 1407 it became a prison. It is said that the man who supervised its construction became its first prisoner! The Bicêtre was a lunatic asylum before it became a prison from which convicts were sent to the galleys chained together, twenty-six at a time.

The galleys, both ancient and modern, were themselves a sort of prison. Few of the Greek or Roman galley slaves were actual felons, but both France and Italy (and the Papal State) used galleys as punishment for both minor and major offenders not condemned to execution or transportation, up to the first part of the nineteenth century. The last consignment of prisoners went from the Bicêtre to the galleys in 1835, and any convicted man who had strength to work an oar might be condemned to them, even an old man or a cripple. In both the ancient and the

9

modern galleys, the prisoners were chained to their places, ate and slept there, and the only means of discipline was the whip.

As laws multiplied and crimes increased, it became a growing problem to know what to do with petty offenders, the "rogues and vagabonds" who seem to have proliferated as the Middle Ages came to their end. The answer seemed to be what were known variously as workhouses or houses of correction. In 1553 the Bridewell, a "fine and stately" house built in London by Henry VIII to entertain the visiting Charles V, was turned into such a depository for the "vagabond, idle, and dissolute." From that time (though it was not confirmed by Parliament until 1720) such institutions have been known in England as Bride-wells. Amsterdam followed suit, though not until nearly fifty years later, then various cities of Germany and Switzerland. France did not follow until 1650; then it was largely a Protestant movement and hence not supported by the State. All these workhouses were occupied by the insane, orphans, and the poor (who entered voluntarily at times of dire need), as well as by petty criminals. Amsterdam's was the best: it paid a small wage to inmates who worked at such tasks as rasping dyewood; it had a doctor in residence; held religious services; and taught reading, writing, and arithmetic to the illiterate.

It must be remembered that in nearly all early prisons, especially in England, the wardenship was a perquisite, bought or bestowed or inherited, and the warden (or governor as he is known in England) ran the prison as a business enterprise for his own profit. We shall see a good deal more of this and its effects a little later when we view prisons as they existed just before the first surge of reform at the end of the eighteenth century, but it is of interest to note that even so early there was some concern for the condition of the prisoners. A committee of the House of Commons reported in 1593:

"The Queen hath been given to understand that some that receive grants for the keeping of gaols [or "jails," as the Americans spell it] and others to whom the charge of gaols is assigned have leased them out at exceeding great rents or other profits. Thus their assigns are constrained to exact excessive prices for victuals, bedding, fire, fees of irons [the prisoner had to pay even for the shackles that bound him!], and other things from poor prisoners, who for want of means to satisfy these unreasonable demands, do perish through famine; for they remain in prison a long time after they are discharged of the principal cause of their commitment only for lack of ability to defray the great sums exacted of them for such intolerable impositions."

It was to be a long time before anything was done to answer this just complaint of Queen Elizabeth's. The position of the pauper prisoner, without friends or relatives to help keep him alive, was a frightening one. Not only must he somehow pay for the miserable food which was the best he could hope for, for the straw on which he lay in his chains, for the fire to keep him from freezing, but no matter what the original term of his sentence had been, he could not leave until he had paid his debt to his jailer. Many prisoners lived by begging alone, either by the largess of visitors or those who passed by the contributions box fastened outside the prison, or by actually going out into the streets by day with an appeal to the public for food or money.

Nevertheless, the number of prisons continued to grow. In England, as early as the twelfth century, when the only prisons were still the dungeon or keep of the king's or the lord's castle, the Assize of Clarendon ordered every

11

county to build its own jail; but no county seems to have paid much attention, except Sussex and Gloucester. Gradually certain buildings in London were recognized as the particular places of detention for specified courts. Thus, the courts at Westminster used the Marshalsea, but mostly for debtors and those guilty of contempt of court; the Court of Chancery used the Fleet; the Tower was for prisoners of state. These were all, we must not forget, merely places of detention until the convict paid his fine—or went to the gallows.

In no prison, jail, or workhouse was there any attempt at segregation by age or sex or any other criterion—except in Renaissance Italy, where instead of the usual mixed dormitories, there were cells in which prisoners were kept in solitary confinement, the avowed object being to separate those of noble birth from common prisoners!

It was not until 1703 that Pope Clement XI founded his famous Hospice of St. Michael in Rome, for the housing of boy criminals under the age of twenty and of incorrigible and disobedient boys sent there by their parents. This was a giant step upward, inasmuch as it separated the young from hardened older criminals, but it was far from what we could understand today as a reformatory, let alone a "boys' town." The prisoners spun and knitted, chained to their benches by one foot, in utter silence, while a priest read aloud to them from pious works. Any infraction of rules was punished by flogging. At night they slept alone in small brick cells. This became the pattern for prisons for "juvenile delinquents" for two centuries to come. The *Maison de Force,* founded in 1627 in Ghent (then in an Austrian province of Flanders), was a house of correction, but for adult offenders as well as juveniles. Vicompte J. J. P. Vilain, its director in 1775, copied St. Michael's in that the prisoners worked in common, but were separated at night. Amsterdam, again in the lead,

12

established a real reformatory for women in 1593, but it was a long time before any other city or nation followed suit.

"Rogues and vagabonds" and petty offenders were, indeed, throughout this period, consigned to jails and workhouses simply to get them off the roads and out of the gutters. Though in a sense one may say they were being punished for their offenses by imprisonment, usually no definite term was set; man, woman, or child merely stayed on until somehow he or she had means to pay any fines, to reimburse the keeper for the exorbitant expenses of prison life, and to demonstrate some means of self-support —which in most cases meant never. Unless such a prisoner escaped, he was likely to die in prison. Petty offenses were still for the most part punished by flogging or some other form of physical chastisement. Occasionally some enlightened person in power—like the Quaker William Penn in Pennsylvania and West Jersey—abolished corporal punishment for crime except for murder; but, as was the case after Penn died and his son succeeded him, such innovations were short-lived.

It was the end of the eighteenth century, with the industrial revolution beginning in real earnest, before any government thought seriously of making imprisonment itself a penalty for crime. Occasionally, before that, men had in some places been sentenced to prison to expiate their offenses, with no other penalty attached (we have seen some instances of this), but in general, anywhere in Europe or later in the English colonies in America, this was an unfamiliar concept.

By the time the eighteenth century neared its end, however, the concept was becoming increasingly familiar. Concurrently with the crowding of all sorts of prisons and prison-substitutes with men and women (and small children) sentenced for specific terms or for life, there arose

13

the first great wave of reform, the Quakers being the pioneers.

But before we tell the story of the early reformers, let us take a look at the conditions which inspired their revulsion and their zeal.

3

Up to the present advanced philosophy of penology, there have been in modern times three principal schools of thought. The first was the Classical School, voiced by the early reformer Cesare Beccaria in 1846, which considered imprisonment "a problem in exact justice" and sought to tailor the exact penalty to fit not the criminal, but the crime. The next was the Neo-Classical School, which modified Beccaria's teaching by measuring out the penalty in proportion to the "social responsibility" of the criminal. Then came the so-called Italian School of Cesare Lombroso and his followers (though the Marchese de Beccaria was of course Italian too), according to which the criminal is an ascertainable physical type, who must be treated until he lives up to the social standards of his time and place. From this there is a direct line to the current belief of penologists that the purpose of punishment is not to wreak vengeance on the offender or even primarily to deter him from further crime, but to rehabilitate him and make him into a law-abiding citizen. (There is no connection between current penological views and the exaggerated dependence of Lombroso on his—largely imaginative—criminal stigmata.)

In so far as the prison in the eighteenth century was based on any principle at all, except pure vengeance and the satisfaction of social anger, it was naturally Beccaria's views which influenced it. But the actual institutions which had grown out of the kings' and nobles' private

14

prisons of the past were, at the beginning of the period of reform, little affected by any philosophy at all.

Let us look at a typical prison of this period and select England, not because English prisons were among the worst, but because they were among the best.

In the first place, as has been said, the prison was a private business enterprise, given as a favor to or bought by an enterprising man who expected to run it like any other business venture, and to make as much profit out of it as he possibly could. When he died, he could will his lease to his heirs like any other of his assets. Frequently leases descended from father to son for several generations. Most frequently the lessor did not run the prison himself, but sublet the privilege; hence the lessee was even more set on making enough money to pay the original holder and have something left over for himself.

This did not necessarily mean that either lessor or lessee was cruel. Both might be considered callous by our standards, but it was an impersonal callousness sanctioned by all the mores of their time and hence not even realized. Even a naturally kind and tenderhearted man would see no injustice in starving or freezing his prisoners if they could not pay for their own keep. Norah Loft, in her novel, *The House at Old Vine*, has a passage which illustrates this admirably. (The date is supposed to be 1645, but the condition is equally true of the following century.) A rural jail keeper is speaking:

"When you get a chap . . . what is tried and found guilty, but ain't delivered from gaol by way of a whipping or the stocks, what can I do? I don't run a free lodging house, do I? Porridge, and a bit of bread now and then, is the best I can do, and at that I'm out of pocket. . . . There's another thing—straw. Cheap, but it ain't free. . . . You clump down your good money to be gaoler

15

year after year, and you make just enough profit to keep yourself alive from them waiting a trial that can afford to pay for comforts."

Less amiable keepers saw no reason to provide even the "porridge and a bit of bread." And this was a rural jail for minor offenders. The kindly old keeper never had to deal with a murderer or a professional highwayman. Because there was no central authority, legislation ran far ahead, as we shall see, of actual conditions. In the middle of the eighteenth century, the typical English prison—Newgate, for example—was no better than, say, the private prison run in old days by the Bishop of Ely, where the prisoners lay on the stone floor with spiked iron collars fastened on their necks and heavy iron bars across their legs: in some ways it was worse. The fee system, whereby the prisoners must pay for every decency or alleviation—edible food, straw to sleep on, water to drink, even enough air to breathe (in various categories known technically as garnish, footing, or chummage)—or go without them and survive as best they could, or succumb, made of most prisons only a sure means to slow death. The mortality in prisons was five times that of the free population. At a time when all life expectancy was much less than it is in the civilized world today, that of middle-aged convicts was reduced by thirty-six years if they had to spend more than a short time as prisoners.

One reason for this was "gaol fever," which was malignant typhoid or typhus. Both rats and fleas abounded, and the sick slept cheek by jowl with the well and infected them. In the scientific innocence of the day, this was considered a disease merely bred by prisons themselves, and hence unavoidable and incurable. Few prisons had infirmaries, and if they did, the infirmary was merely a bare room where the sick lay on moldy straw side by side, with little or no medical treatment, and without concern for the nature of the illness of any of them.

The typical prison consisted of large common rooms, where men, women, and children lived, ate, and slept without the slightest attempt at segregation. Privacy was a thing unheard of, except for rich prisoners of state, who lived on the inside (in the Tower, for example) in much the same state as on the outside, with their servants, their curtains and hangings and furniture and even their silver plate installed from their homes, their meals prepared by their own cooks or brought in to them from outside, with extra delicacies provided by friends and well-wishers.

But these were rare exceptions. The average poor prisoner—and most prisoners were poor, if not penniless— knew no such luxuries. They were dressed in the rags they had brought with them; they slept without bedding on the hard floor, however freezing the temperature. Though in some cases meager portions of bad bread and dirty water were dispensed to them, in others they were entirely dependent for food on begging on the streets or from visitors, if they or their families had no money.

There were always visitors, but they were not earnest, social-minded people bent on alleviating distress. They were sightseers, "slummers," jaded gentry who visited the prisons for the thrill of a spectacle, just as they visited the lunatic asylums—or as we would visit a zoo. Fortunately for the wretched pauper prisoners, these visitors knew they would be expected to provide a few coins in return for the entertainment.

Neglected children, respectable debtors, what we would consider petty offenders who had stolen a loaf from sheer hunger or been tempted by a bright ribbon owned by some slavey's mistress, were thrown into the closest contact, twenty-four hours a day, with habitual criminals, murderers, burglars, prostitutes, consumptives, syphilitics. There was not a place or a minute in which anyone could be alone.

Every prison had its kangaroo court, where the judges were the worst and most brutal of the inmates, and where the unhappy newcomer had to supply "furnish" to buy drinks, or else run the gantlet, stripped naked, and be viciously beaten. For one thing that was supplied in quantity—for a price—was liquor. The keepers were licensed like tavern owners. If a man had the money to pay, no one could blame him from seeking the only release from his surroundings in drunkenness.

The filth was unspeakable—the place was literally never cleaned. Sanitary facilities were so primitive as to be practically nonexistent. Vermin of every sort abounded; hungry rats gnawed at sleepers; everybody had lice as a matter of course, since nobody ever washed. It is no wonder that the stench was unbearable. How the visitors from the outer world stood it is a problem; they and the visiting officials carried bouquets or pomanders as judges did when prisoners were brought from the prison for trial. A century before, Sir Francis Bacon had ordered that prisoners be "aired before brought forth," but even after an hour's airing they still offended sensitive nostrils. This was in an age when standards of cleanliness were considerably less than they are in our antiseptic time.

These wretched creatures suffered not only from malnutrition and dirt and the diseases of dirt, but they were also easy victims to the diseases caused by lack of light and of sufficient air. Windows were few and small, and the inner rooms were often windowless. They seldom left the prison except perhaps to beg in groups under the eye of a watchful guard—for releases were very infrequent. So far as comfort was concerned, they might just as well have

18

been thrown into the dungeons and oubliettes of the private prisons of the past.

In such a society, made up of the ignorant, the poor, and the criminally inclined, and during a period of general brutality, one can imagine to what the comparatively innocent were exposed. Sexual promiscuity was taken as a matter of course. Prostitutes plied their trade, but the mentally retarded servant girl from the country who had filched a petticoat from her mistress's wardrobe was also at the mercy of any man among her fellow prisoners. Children of seven or eight (and remember that a debtor's pauper dependents often moved in with him) could stare wide-eyed and gain a quick education.

In the crowding and confusion, quarrels were endemic, especially since those who could afford it had access to plenty of alcohol. Obscenity and profanity were the common speech. The noise was deafening—shrieks, shouts, angry tirades, drunken song—and fights broke out constantly. Often they were fights to the death.

The English prison of the eighteenth century had just one advantage over that of the Continent. English prisoners were not tortured. It is not strange that Mirabeau described the Bicêtre, in Paris, as "a hospital for infecting the sick and a prison for breeding crimes."

With the exception of William Penn's abortive "Great Law" of 1682 which replaced corporal punishment with prisons that were to be "free as to fees, food, and lodging," and which was replaced in 1718 by the reintroduction of English criminal law (the day after Penn died), conditions were not much better in the American colonies. One Connecticut town, for instance, used an abandoned copper mine as a prison; in Maine the prison cells were pits with grating at the top. In Simsbury, Connecticut, the prisoners lay at night with their feet under iron bars and chains leading from their necks to the ceiling beams. Yet even in such prisons there were complaints that the inmates "reveled and rioted"!

One reason for the atrocious conditions was that, as it became increasingly common to make imprisonment the sole punishment for an offense, the inadequate buildings formerly used to hold offenders until their trials were converted into long-time depositories for convicted criminals. Another was that under the leasing system even the sublessor was often an absentee keeper; he in turn let his privilege or hired men cheaply to do the actual work of running the prison. As a matter of course, these final figures in the chain of command were not likely to be of very high caliber. They made little, and their only interest was to make more. They were therefore wide open for bribery and corruption. The consequence was glaring inequality in the treatment of their charges. Favoritism was purchasable, and where even in a common prison some lucky highwayman en route to the gallows might live in comfort, with visits from his doxy to while away his hours, in exchange for presents to the keeper from his takings before he was caught, the wretched bungling pickpocket who had been unsuccessful at his trade, and had nothing with which to bribe, paid for the highwayman's privileges by total deprivation.

The vast majority of the prisoners were completely idle, years on end. In a few instances convicts might be hired out to private contractors, and occasionally some prosperous inmate might hire a penniless one to be his servant. In the past it had been much more common to hire prisoners out, the wages going to the authorities, but as the industrial system changed, this became less profitable. In some prisons "idle labor" or "made labor" became established—the treadmill and the crank. They, with stone-breaking and picking oakum (digging out the fibers with one's fingernails from old, tar-soaked rope—it was used to caulk ships, and oakum-picking still obtains in some European prisons), later became universal in England as elsewhere. In the eighteenth century they were common on the Continent and in America. That Connecticut mine-prison, for example, had a treadwheel and sometimes woman prisoners were made to walk it with the men, as a disciplinary punishment.

The crank was a variation of the treadmill. Instead of walking, one stood on a platform and turned a crank with one's hands. In some prisons inmates had to "earn" their meals by so many revolutions beforehand—1800 for breakfast, 4500 for dinner. The average requirement was 10,000 revolutions a day, and if the day's quota had not been made, the prisoner had to continue turning it after dark in his cell. (This, however, was a later refinement, when early reforms had substituted cells for common rooms.) The resistance of the crank could be set—ten pounds of resistance for a man, five pounds for a boy.

The whole outrageous situation was, as has been pointed out, a direct result of the industrial revolution. When mass labor in factories replaced hand labor at home, a landless, jobless, often homeless proletariat was created. The growing number of vagrants and "idle rogues" had already led to the establishment of workhouses, sometimes called houses of correction. The distinction between them and ordinary jails gradually disappeared. The prisons for long-term felons, filled to overflowing now that imprisonment itself was to become the general punishment for crime, failed completely to adapt to the new conditions. This was true both in Great Britain and on the Continent. In France it was Mirabeau himself, who spoke so scathingly of the Bicêtre, who had initiated imprisonment as expiation by the Code of 1794. Once the idea had been born, it grew rapidly; in England imprisonment became the most common punishment even when transportation (first to America, then to Australia) was at its height. Ever since the days of Sumer there had been class differentiations in the penalties for crime. In the late eighteenth century it was open and unabashed. As Max Grünhut has said, "The same facts had different meanings for different classes. . . . Imprisonment became the chief punishment throughout the western world at the very moment when the economic foundation of the house of correction was destroyed by industrial changes."

The time was ripe and overripe for reform. It came.

4

Before we go on to the story of the first reforms, legislative and individual, there are two more aspects of the eighteenth-century penal system that call for consideration. The history of the hulks (mostly in England but with repercussions elsewhere) and the story of transportation to penal colonies will carry us in chronology beyond the point we have reached in the account of ordinary prisons, but we shall come back to the early reformers when we have had a comprehensive view of all the evils they were bent on abolishing or alleviating. Both Elizabeth Fry and John Howard, the two most prominent of these pioneers, concerned themselves with the plight of prisoners consigned to transportation or confined to the floating prisons known as hulks.

The system of transporting convicted criminals (or political dissidents) either to colonies of the transporting country or to isolated districts of the country itself (e.g., Russia to Siberia) grew out of the age-old custom of exile or banishment. We do not know certainly whether the most ancient civilizations practiced it, but the probability is that they did. Perhaps offending members of the tribe were cast out to die even in the Old Stone Age.

In ancient Greece and Rome the custom was universal. Most of those so banished were rebels or the leaders of losing factions in civil conflict or political offenders whom for some reason it was inexpedient to kill outright. History is full of the names of famous men, from Alcibiades to Ovid, who were banished from their homelands for a term or forever. (The Celts were also great banishers, from Gaul to Scotland.) But gradually, in Rome at least, criminals, as well as captives of war and the smaller fry among political offenders, were consigned to remote mines or quarries. Sometimes they were condemned to the galleys, never to see their homes or loved ones again but chained to their seats until they died of exhaustion and flogging or were killed in battle—the oarsmen, from their exposed position, were always the first to fall to the enemy.

From sending a man to eke out his existence as best he could in some distant barbarous land, or sending him to slave until his death in a mine or a galley, it was only a step to sending him to a prison camp in a colony. The *ancient* colonies were not transformed into penal institutes; the best of the vigorous young went out as pioneers to extend the property and glory of their homelands. Rome gave farms in the colonies to discharged veterans. However, with the rise of modern colonialism, the parent countries began to treat their colonies as so many dumping grounds for their own undesirables.

A note of clarification: Transportation is sometimes spoken of as deportation. According to contemporary usage, deportation is expulsion of an alien from the country in which he has been residing—usually his return to his native land; transportation applies to the sending of natives to a colony or distant part of their own country.

All of the great colonial powers of the Modern Age practiced transportation of criminals to some extent. Portugal did not abandon the system until World War II.

Theirs was a relatively easy system, however; the convicts were sent to Angola, in Africa, but there lived as free men, mingling with the free Portuguese settlers. There are those who see in this hereditary strain of the white settlers one of the background causes of the current bitter struggle of the Africans of Angola to throw off the yoke of the colonizers and achieve their independence.

Holland used the Dutch East Indies as a depository for unwanted nationals; Italy, various islands off its coast (under the Fascist State, the Lipari Islands, north of Sicily, were especially favored for political prisoners). In neither case was there anything like the relative lenity of Angola; the penal regime was harsh and brutal.

But the three countries in which transportation of convicts was most outstanding as a feature of their criminal law were France, Russia, and England.

To this day, underworld French argot for either a prison or a penal camp is *bagne*, evidence of their direct descent from the galleys. In 1791 the French government ordered that all men convicted of a felony for the second time be transported for life. Madagascar was the place chosen, but then the Napoleonic Wars intervened and this project was never put into effect. Transportation was not revived until 1851—which takes us again beyond the eighteenth century, to a time when England was already in the process of abolishing the system. In that year Louis Napoleon signed a decree which re-established transportation, with Algeria and French Guiana named as places of exile.

The decree, however, was declared illegal, though the first boatload of prisoners had already gone out in 1852. Two years later it was passed again, legally, and Algeria was omitted—a fortunate proviso, in view of the present situation there. The prisoners were taken from among the inmates of the overcrowded hulks, and for another seventy years the Toulon hulks were in use as waiting places for those to be sent on the semiannual journey. For a while New Caledonia, in the South Pacific, was one of the designated penal colonies, but this was finally abandoned and Guiana became the only one.

It was a journey into hell. French Guiana had never been successful as a free colony. Most of it is tropical jungle, still partly unexplored, and the torrid climate is unbearable to Europeans. They died like flies, and they were not replaced. Negro slaves were imported; they staged a successful revolt and escaped into the forest, where their descendants still live. Cayenne, the capital and only town of consequence, was known as a pesthole, especially in the days before modern medicine. A good part of the meager remaining free population was made up of Chinese merchants who had no interest in the colony as such.

As a colony it was a failure; as a dump for unwanted convicts it was ideal to the bureaucratic mind. Barracks were established on the mainland, and three offshore islands, Royale, St. Joseph, and Île du Diable (Devil's Island) were set aside for "desperate" and incorrigible men. The three are known as the Safety Islands—an ironical name. Actually the first prisoner to be incarcerated on Devil's Island, which is only 3600 square feet of rock, was the famous Captain Alfred Dreyfus, who spent nearly five years there, from 1894 to 1899, under close guard, until his vindication—but he was not the last. The island was reserved for political prisoners.

The penal colony in French Guiana has well been called "the dry guillotine" by René Belbenoit, a prisoner with a remarkable history of escapes, who exposed its horrors in two books. The prisoners worked from dawn to dark, building roads or cutting rubber in the jungle, naked to the waist, assailed by flies and mosquitoes and chiggers. At night vampire bats drank their blood. Dressed in red and

25

white striped uniforms to make them conspicuous, ill fed on moldy food, drinking polluted water, cursed and beaten by the only kind of guards who would be likely to accept service in such a spot, they dragged out their miserable months and years. There was no segregation. A large part of the prison population was made up of hardened habitual criminals, and every new man found himself eagerly fought over as prey for the sexual attentions of men confirmed in homosexuality by lack of normal partners. From 1885 to 1902, women prisoners were also sent to Guiana, but the resultant "scandals," riots, and murders ended that experiment. Even without that incentive, assaults and murders of prisoners by their fellows and by guards were endemic. There was no religious instruction, no education, no attempt at providing any sort of recreation. There was never even a mess hall—the men ate sitting on the ground, their plates on their knees. Sex, gambling, and liquor when they could get it were the only alleviations of their lot.

It is no wonder that a sentence to Guiana, whatever its ostensible length, became in reality a life sentence. Heat, brutality, hard labor chopping hardwood (and most of the convicted thieves were city products unused to manual labor), malnutrition and the consequent dysentery, fever and tropical diseases of all sorts soon did their work, which may have been the more or less deliberate intention. It is estimated that half of the prisoners died in their first year in the colony, a quarter more during their second year, and only a tenth of them lived as long as five years —and five years was the lightest of the sentences under which they were transported, many being sentenced to twenty years, or for life. Of the 80,000 men sent to Guiana, 87 per cent died as prisoners.

Moreover, if a man lived to serve his full sentence, though he was free he was still an exile, a *libéré*. This penalty of *doublage* was not even told him till his release. Without money, with practically no economic opportunities, he was expected somehow to earn his living. About all there was to do was to gather rubber or hunt butterflies for sale. *Libérés* had to serve the same time in exile as their original sentence, or, if that was for more than seven years, for life. They were not allowed to enter the town of Cayenne for the first ten years after their prison sentences had expired but were obliged to live in makeshift *libéré* villages. Few of them ever saw France again.

In addition, there were the so-called *relégués,* undesirables who had received four convictions for petty larceny or the like. They were simply banished for life from France to Guiana, without prison sentences, and were left there to survive or rot—or escape. They ended up in jungle barracks, which became dens of perversion and squalor.

It is only fair to add that another transported convict, Francis Lagrange, called Belbenoit's account exaggerated and sensational. Everything Belbenoit says, he affirms, is true of some periods and some parts of the penal colony, but "it was not the policy of the French government to dispatch prisoners to Guiana in order to torture and kill them. [It was] no worse than most prisons and in some important respects considerably better." Nothing, he agrees, can justify the treatment of the "incorrigibles" on St. Joseph Island, and his picture of universal corruption is even worse than Belbenoit's. His recollection of the fifteen-day voyage, with 150 men locked in a guarded cage and allowed only a half-hour of fresh air and exercise a day, is as strong an indictment of the system as any made by others.

Naturally, every prisoner had but one thought in mind —escape. Escape was easy, but it nearly always failed (except for "big" criminals who could bribe lavishly). The captured *évadé* was brought back for further punishment

27

—or, if he was not captured, he died in the jungle or drowned in shark-infested waters. If he reached one of the adjoining countries, he might be worked until he was no longer profitable and then turned in for a meager reward. Indeed, his own comrades, themselves doubtless planning escape, were eager to betray him in return for some slight privilege.

After Mrs. Blair Niles, and then Belbenoit, disclosed the horrors of Guiana, the French government made a diplomatic gesture. It was not only the unspeakable treatment of the prisoners which they had revealed, but also the favoritism, corruption, and graft of the guards and officials, which one or two good governors had found themselves powerless to prevent. Ostensibly, after 1867, no Europeans were condemned to Guiana, but only natives of France's overseas colonies presumably better fitted for life in the tropics—though Belbenoit categorically denies this. In 1938 the government publicly announced that it was ending the system; that those already sentenced would serve out their terms, but no more criminals would be transported. According to Belbenoit, a thousand new prisoners were dispatched to Guiana after this declaration, up to 1941 when he wrote. Transportation was finally and definitely abolished by the Free French government after World War II. There are still about a hundred ex-convicts living in French Guiana.

Back to the eighteenth century, and to perhaps the most notorious of all transportation systems—that of Russia.

In 1753 Czarist Russia abolished capital punishment, and all persons who would previously have been executed were condemned instead to hard labor for life in Siberia. The Island of Sakhalin, in the North Pacific, and the Solovetski Islands, in the Arctic Ocean, were also used as places of imprisonment; the monastery prison in the latter, in use from the sixteenth century until 1905, was revived as a prison by the Soviets.

A good part of the Czarist prisoners sent to Siberia never reached it; they died on the way. They walked every foot of the thousands of miles, often in deep snow; these were the so-called *étapes*, or marches. Prisoners were divided into two categories: those who at the end of their sentences could either go home or remain as free colonists, and those considered "dead to the world," with half their heads shaved to distinguish them, who had no hope except to toil in the mines until their lives ended. These people had not only lost all civil rights but were considered legally dead; their property was confiscated, and if their families did not accompany them, which was most often the case, their wives were free to remarry.

For the ordinary criminal in the first category, life was hard but endurable. For the political prisoners (nobody has estimated how many of the million or more exiles to Siberia under the Czars were politicals) it was almost beyond endurance. Seventy years ago or more George Kennan, in his *Siberia and the Exile System,* laid bare to the world all the terrors of the regime. As was the case in the Nazi concentration camps, the common criminal was the top dog. The political prisoners, whether they rebelled or not, were subjected to the harshest discipline and to periodical roundups in which they lost what small privileges they had or were redistributed to other prisons and the mines attached to them.

Everybody in the Western world, at least, knows that the transportation and exile system of Czarist times has been continued by the U.S.S.R., and that the overwhelming majority of those so condemned are dissidents or "deviationists" of one kind or another or non-Communists from the satellite countries. What is not known is just

29

what the conditions are like in their penal labor camps in Siberia, which are closed territories to foreigners. Anti-Communists portray them as places of horror and degradation, worse than the worst of the Czarist prisons; pro-Communists insist that they are scenes of enlightened penology, with no hardship worse than is suffered by all pioneers into undeveloped country. It is a controversy which is at present insusceptible to settlement. In any case, it will be discussed further when we consider the state of penology in all the world today.

We come now to the transportation system in England. The gradual change toward the end of the eighteenth century to the concept of imprisonment as punishment for crime had the natural effect, as we have seen, of badly overcrowding what prisons there were. The hulks, which will be described later, took off some of this pressure, but soon they too became overcrowded. It was then that it occurred to the authorities that the colonies would be an excellent place in which to get rid of the Mother Country's criminals and at the same time provide free labor for the voluntary colonists.

The first place they tried was Sierra Leone, on the west coast of Africa, but unlike the French in Guiana, England did not want an execution chamber disguised as a penal colony, and it was soon abandoned because of the tropical heat. (Belbenoit says "questions and matters of prison systems are not a thing of public concern" in France; he is understandably unfair, but it is true that the English have always taken a more responsible attitude toward the treatment of criminals.)

The most natural destination for transported convicts was first the West Indies and then the mainland of British North America. As early as 1619 James I had ordered "a hundred dissolute persons" to be sent to Virginia. Some convicts had been sent there from the time of Elizabeth I.

(Some of the First Families of Virginia must still be descended from these exiles and their successors, a matter about which they would doubtless prefer to be ignorant!) In such places as Barbados and Jamaica, however, where Negro slavery was the prevailing feature of the economy, there was small demand for the labor of unskilled and recalcitrant white criminals. Soon transportation was confined to the mainland colonies, particularly of the South. These transported men and women—mostly petty criminals, but including also vagrants and the general riffraff which had stuffed the workhouses beyond capacity—were sold into practical slavery or peonage for the term of their sentences, going to work as servants or farm laborers, for the most part, for the settled residents. It must be pointed out that, however disagreeable the voyage and harsh the servitude, the exiles to America were not confined in prisons, and after their sentences expired many of them remained. Some became solid citizens and even intermarried with the free population; others added to the criminal class of their new homeland. It was a very different experience from that of being transported to Australia, which happened later. (France also exiled a few criminals and prostitutes to her American colonies—as witness Manon, banished to the "desert" of Louisiana!)

The whole system of transportation to America came to an abrupt end in 1776, with the revolt of the colonies and the successful American Revolution. For a while England tried again to make room for its convicted criminals in prisons and hulks, but it was impossible. Then, providentially, Australasia was discovered by Captain Cook and taken over by England.

The convicts arrived in Australia almost as soon as the first free colonists. The first boatload was sent to Botany Bay in 1787, with Arthur Phillip as the first governor.

After the incredibly long voyage in a sailing ship, the

first prisoners landed in an utterly undeveloped land. They were left to build their own barracks, to cultivate the virgin soil as best they could, to get by somehow until supplies arrived from England. They were not farmers or builders; they were unskilled, flabby, ill-nourished thieves and vagabonds. Most of them suffered from scurvy. Then smallpox broke out and killed them by the score. They were attacked constantly by the natives, and they had neither arms nor military experience. It is surprising that any of them were still alive when relief and supplies finally reached them in 1790. It took eight months to make the journey.

After that, condemned criminals were transported regularly from England to Australasia for nearly a century.

Some years ago, an enterprising outfit bought the old Australian prison ship *Success* and sent her on a worldwide tour to all the harbors of the civilized world, as a sort of floating museum. To visit that ship was an object lesson in what the dreadful voyage must have been like. One of its features was a cage in which insubordinate passengers were kept. It had a sort of horizontal saw, fastened to the bars at either end, known as the "tiger's jaw," so arranged that a chained prisoner would stand with his chin just above it. With every motion of the waves the "jaw" would come up and "bite" him. That was a refinement; for the most part the fist and the whip were sufficient means of discipline.

All the worst characteristics of the noisome prisons already described appeared in a nautical version of the floating hells known as convict ships—filth, vermin, insufficient and inadequate food and clothing, complete lack of privacy, brutality from the soldiers who acted as guards, kangaroo courts, fights often ending in murder and always marked by bloodshed. Women as well as men were transported, and there was no separation of the sexes. In fact, the crew drew lots when the ship started, to take eight-month mistresses for themselves; the rest were locked with the men in the dark, fetid hold, and many of the sanguinary quarrels arose when a man took his choice of a woman whom some other man wanted. Most of these women were prostitutes or had lived the promiscuous lives of the degraded pauper, and those who were "drawn" in the crew lottery were envied—they would breathe fresh air and get more to eat (for the private ships' chandlers who grew rich on the trade cheated everybody, but cheated the prisoners worse than they did the crew). But heaven help the occasional girl unused to such a life who was condemned to transportation! (In 1820 Elizabeth Fry secured separate cells for the women—for which many did not thank her!) Chains, starvation, beatings, disease, blows, curses, mingled with loud ribaldry and desperate plots for mutiny, some of which were defeated only by shooting the ringleaders.

Once arrived in Australia, most of the prisoners were detained in Botany Bay, though there were also prison camps at Port Macquarie and in Tasmania. The "twice condemned," convicted men who committed new crimes in Australia, were sent to Norfolk Island, a place of horror before Captain Alexander Maconochie (all the officials were naval officers) inaugurated his famous reforms, which will be explained later.

With one exception, the early governors tried hard to mitigate the fate of their charges. Captain King opened an orphanage, married off couples who were good prospects for rehabilitation, and gave them homesteads. Captain Lachlan Macquarie managed to get the government to send out prisoners' families to join them, and he recruited girls from English reformatories to come to Australia and marry bachelor prisoners. When Botany Bay was transformed from a penal settlement into a colony (free settlement officially began in 1816), he even made one ex-convict a judge! The exception was the notorious Captain William Bligh. Eighteen years after the mutiny on the *Bounty,* he became governor, only to meet another mutiny. So harsh was his rule that the entire populace, including his own soldiers, the few free colonists, and the convicts, rose against him, locked him in his own house, and succeeded in having him forcibly deported.

The convicts, no matter what their age or physical condition, did hard grueling labor with long hours. They broke and cultivated the ground, dug in the mines, burned lime, did every sort of heavy task necessary in a newly opened country. Their guards were always brutal and often cruel. They lived in bare barracks, ate poor and scanty food, underwent heavy hardships, and of course there were none of the alleviations of imprisonment in existence today, any more than there were in prisons at home. But the Australian penal colonies were never the hell on earth that French Guiana was.

For one thing, from the mid-nineteenth century on, a system of quasi-parole known as "ticket of leave" was introduced, by which a man who had served a certain portion of his time satisfactorily was given conditional freedom under supervision. His lot was very different from that of the French *libéré.* The vast majority of convicts transported to Australia remained there after expiration of their sentences and were lost in the general population. Many of them made good, some achieved economic and social stature. It is no secret that many of the "old" Australian families have a transported convict or two among their ancestors. (Perhaps the fact that the first permanent settlers in Australia came largely from the London proletariat accounts for the cockney accent of Australians to this day!)

34

What brought an end to transportation of criminals to Australia was not prison reform, but wool, wheat, and gold. When gold was discovered in New South Wales in 1851, it brought the same influx into the land as it brought to California in 1849. Many who did or did not find gold stayed on to raise sheep or wheat. The first free colonists, who had found convicts, and later ticket-of-leave men, a ready and cheap source of needed labor, and who were called "emancipists" because they advocated the absorption of ex-convicts instead of their repatriation, were countered by these newcomers, who as "exclusivists" wanted the penal camps and the whole system of transportation wiped out.

After 1840 no new prisoners were sent to New South Wales. From 1847 on, the actual prison term was served in England, and only ticket-of-leave men were sent to Australia for the rest of their terms. In 1853, it was ordered that four years of penal servitude equaled seven years of transportation, and that no one sentenced for less than fourteen years should be transported. Transportation had practically died out by 1864, though until 1867 a few convicts were sent to serve part of their terms in West Australia, and as late as 1890 (though Australia by then had her own penal system) the home country was still supporting some leftovers from Botany Bay. Today Port Arthur, Tasmania, which once held some 8500 prisoners, is a ghost town; its prison, a ruin. All that is left is the Island of the Dead, where convicts who died in prison were cast into a lime pit for burial.

With the improvement of conditions, transportation everywhere lost the terror it was supposed to inspire to make it a deterrent from crime. It is significant that France, where the terror was most justified, was the last to abandon the system. A few South American countries

35

still exile criminals (and political enemies) to prisons in islands off their coasts, but as a recognized method of punishment it is to all intents and purposes dead.

Belief in its efficacy died hard. Lombroso still considered it an excellent means of punitive treatment. But it has no place in modern penology. As Harry Elmer Barnes and Negley K. Teeters say, it "has been proved a ghastly failure wherever it has been tried."

5

When, in 1776, because of the American Revolution, it no longer became possible for England to transport its criminals and undesirables to America, there was nothing to do but to find room for them somewhere in England. Nobody foresaw then that Australia would soon supply a happy solution.

Then somebody in officialdom had a bright idea. Why not recondition some old ships, moor them in inland waters, and use them to house convicts who could then be used for public works ashore?

The whole thing was a temporary expedient, renewed from year to year, but it continued, in one form or another, for eighty years or more. At first it was put on a quasi-voluntary basis: prisoners who would formerly have been shipped to America were given their choice between the hulks or hanging; it is needless to say which most of them preferred. From the outset the hulks were designed for "the more severe and effectual punishment of atrocious and daring offenders"—men only. (Actually, many French prisoners of war during the Napoleonic Wars and Americans during the War of 1812 spent up to ten years aboard such moored vessels, but they did no public work, or any other.)

The first of these floating prisons was tied up in the Thames, near the Woolwich Arsenal, and the men worked chiefly at deepening the channel and cleaning the river bed. Later, hulks were moored at Portsmouth and Plymouth, and in Bermuda—which was really a form of transportation. By 1825 there were ten hulks in England and others at various points overseas, with nearly five thousand prisoners in England alone. After Botany Bay was established, the hulks were used to hold men until they could be transported, just as France used her *bagnes* for those condemned to Guiana.

If conditions in English prisons at this time were outrageously bad, those on the hulks were almost beyond description. The same old system of private contract prevailed, with the only consideration the enriching of the contractor at the expense of the wretched prisoners. The Justices of Middlesex County appointed one Duncan Campbell as overseer of the first two hulks (on the Thameside), and he in turn appointed his brother Neil as overseer and went into the business of private exploitation. Popularly the hulks were known as "Campbell's Academy." In actuality he was a slave overseer and the men in his charge were completely at his mercy.

They were marched under guard to work ashore every day, marched back at night. When they were not ashore they were held below decks. The prisoners worked in fetters, guarded by men armed with drawn cutlasses, and were flogged if they were slow or recalcitrant. They ate nothing all day, and it was thought a great privilege that they were allowed to pause occasionally for a minute to drink dirty water from a neighboring ditch. If a man dropped dead, as often happened, he was promptly buried without ceremony—at first on the river bank, later near the Arsenal. It is no surprise that a worker under such conditions was estimated to do only a third of the labor of the same sort which could be expected of a free man. In three years one-eighth of the prisoners died. (This was considered an improvement on transportation, where one-seventh died on the convict ships or in the penal colony during the same length of time.)

Eight out of ten of those who died were listed as having expired from "depression of spirits." When epidemics of "gaol fever" occurred, they were blamed on an infection the victims must have brought from the county jails or from Newgate, though as a matter of fact the prisoners on the hulks did not come to them from either place. There were plenty of rats and fleas on board to account for attacks of typhus and other infectious diseases.

On the hulks there were men of seventy and more, cripples, blind men, lunatics, and up to 1779, boys as young as fourteen. All were required to do a full day's work every day but (sometimes) Sunday, no matter how weak, ill, or incapable they might be. After a while those too badly crippled for heavy labor were set to making a vegetable garden on shore, but it was the officials who ate the vegetables. The men seldom tasted them, and the consequence was that scurvy was endemic.

Campbell was supposed to provide the prisoners with food and clothing. The food consisted of "stinking cheese," bread that was half straw, and dry peas. On two days of the week the men were served cheese and oatmeal only. On four days they had small beer to drink, on the other three they had no liquid but water from the polluted river. It was forbidden to have any food given them from outside.

Friends and relatives were allowed to furnish them with clothes; failing this they went half naked. When a prisoner first came aboard he was given a jacket, a pair of breeches, and a shirt. These were to last him indefinitely, no matter how long his sentence, and even though he worked and slept in them. The official orders were that men must wash every day, shave and change their shirts

38

weekly, but few were able to pay any attention to this impossible demand, and they were all infested with lice.

They slept either in hammocks, or on platforms which during the day were used as tables. On these platforms each man was allotted a space six by two feet, with a mat under him and a thin rug above, unless some friend had provided him with a blanket. The hulks were overcrowded and the men had to sleep spoon fashion. The stench below decks was overwhelming. The ship was never washed, and was never intended to be. Campbell virtuously claimed that he couldn't have the decks washed, lest the men catch cold!

When John Howard first inspected the hulks in 1776, he found that many of the prisoners were obliged to work barefooted because they had no shoes. (It is only fair to add that on his second inspection in 1779 he found improvement in this and a few other respects.)

Once the hulks were established, the same prisoners came back to them again and again. There was good reason for this: a man discharged from the hulks stank; he was lousy; he was usually diseased and always weakened from chains and flogging; and he was shunned by all respectable people. There was nothing for him to do but return to crime, which soon meant another session aboard "Campbell's Academy." There was certainly nothing on board to have rehabilitated him while he was there before—no chaplain, no schooling, no medical service, just irons and the "Black Hole" in the hold if he showed signs of insubordination.

Even in those callous times Campbell's regime began to create a scandal, and before very many more years, Elizabeth Fry, John Howard, and the other early reformers were gaining an audience. In 1779 a hospital ship was established for the seriously ill and hopelessly crippled, and a halfhearted attempt was made at other improvements, including a bit of cleaning. But it was about then that Campbell was also put in charge of new hulks at Portsmouth and Plymouth, where no such refinements were provided. He lasted until 1800, when at last an inspector was appointed by the government. Some attention was paid finally to a rough system of classification; the men were locked in different decks at night and thus separated from the boys (some much younger than the official fourteen) who had been their prey. A visiting chaplain was also appointed, and at least a prayer was said over the dead before they were cast into their hastily dug graves. Irons were made lighter, but there was no change in the system of discipline by corporal punishment. One change was for the worse—most of the public works at the first site had been finished and so many prisoners were idle and left aboard all day without occupation, to brood or quarrel or plot escape or mutiny. Gradually the idea gained favor that the hulks should be outlets for convicted criminals when Botany Bay was full and needed no new recruits, or for the old and handicapped, who nevertheless were set to the hardest manual labor when there was work to do.

By 1825 some real reforms had been initiated. Instead of a mere dumping ground, the hulks became part of a system of central control, with communication between them and the various prisons and penal colonies. Occasionally a long-termer was pardoned outright—though never in the history of the hulks did a man receive a medical discharge, whatever his physical or mental state. In 1823 a special hulk had been built for boys and the age limits tend to make one gasp—boys from six to seventeen were to be sent to it! A system of "promotion" was inaugurated; men whose conduct was good were given sleeping space on the upper deck, where there was air to breathe and the stench was not so bad.

Nevertheless, the hulks could hardly be described as a bed of ease. The guards were not of much higher caliber than the men they guarded, which meant of course that they were open to bribery and all kinds of corruption. The prisoners fought and quarreled, and an occasional murder was taken for granted. There were constant mutinies and attempts to scuttle the ships and escape. None was ever successful, and escapes were rare. It was a rule of terror by the keepers, and also a rule of terror among the prisoners themselves. There were always a few big time professional criminals on board, highwaymen and the like, and they established themselves as "convict kings" who used their weaker and more subservient fellow prisoners as servants. Moreover, the "convict kings" had money, and they could buy favors. There were scandalous tales of important prisoners who came and went as they pleased, had their food and other comforts brought to them from the outside, and in one or two cases usurped the power of the officials placed over them and were the real powers on the hulks to which they had been sent.

As early as 1813 an attempt had been made at some sort of evening classes for illiterates. It failed, but little by little most of the hulks began some kind of school, since half of the convicts were unable to read and write. Sometimes the teacher was the chaplain, occasionally a schoolmaster from the outside, most often a guard or a half-literate fellow convict. Some of the hulks had small collections of books dignified by calling them libraries, but they were mostly pious homilies or religious tracts.

The shoreside workers of course received no pay, though the dockyards made them a tiny allowance. For most of the men, if they were to have any alleviation of the rigorous condition in which they lived it must come by gifts from the free world—the rule against bringing in food seemed to have fallen into abeyance, and wives or mothers

41

might bring with them on the single visit allowed once every three months some decent provender (and even grog) as well as blankets and shoes and shirts. One interesting privilege came to be granted by the 1820's. The quarterly visits took place on a Sunday afternoon, and some of the visitors were allowed to stay overnight—including girl friends! But all this was of small use to the majority of prisoners, who had no relatives or friends or mistresses who were willing or able to bring them anything.

As transportation came to an end, and as new prisons were built on land, the hulks gradually lost their reason for existence. There were few men sentenced to them after 1843, and by 1847 they were thought of as depositories for those who were unfit for transportation. A Parliamentary Report exposed in detail the graft, corruption, disorder, filth, starvation, and ill-treatment which had characterized them from the beginning. Sir Joshua Jebb, chairman of the newly formed Directors of Convict Prisons, decided that any effort to overhaul and reform them would be futile. He ordered that all the 1400 prisoners still on board be transferred to prisons on land.

The abandoned hulks were set afire, the last one in England in 1857. All that remained was the hulk off Bermuda, most of whose prisoners were starved Irish peasants convicted of petty thievery of food during the great potato famine. That too was finally abolished in 1862.

Aside from France and England, "floating prisons" have been used in a few other countries. At least one American state once had a hulk of its own. In 1851 California decided that the time had come when it must have a state prison. While it was casting about for a site, the old Spanish galleon *Euphemia*, which for years had been rotting abandoned in San Pablo Bay near San Francisco, was reconditioned after a fashion, and 150 of the new state's worst criminals were herded aboard her and locked below decks in cells that were designed for 50, four to a cell. There was no ventilation whatever, and they were let out on the deck only in fair weather; sometimes they were kept below for weeks at a time because of fog which would have facilitated escape. The men were in rags, and few of them had even a thin blanket. When the guards had to go down in the morning to feed them, the stench was so bad that only the "most resolute" could endure the duty.

On July 14 (ironically, Bastille Day), 1852, the *Euphemia* was towed to San Quentin Point in Marin County, where General Vallejo had offered (for good return) land for the new prison. The ship was moored alongside, and again the prisoners were left below to "stew in their own juices" on rainy and foggy days and put ashore in good weather to build the prison which was to contain them.

Just when or how another abandoned ship, the *Wabau,* was substituted for the *Euphemia* as the hulk used during the building of San Quentin is difficult to ascertain; perhaps the *Euphemia* merely took the prisoners up to San Quentin Point and they were then transferred. Certainly the *Euphemia* was San Francisco's first city prison, and the *Wabau,* California's first state prison.

Conditions, it need hardly be said, were just as bad on either, eight-by-eight-foot cells and all. Even after the Old Spanish Prison (as the first structure was called) was finished, some of the prisoners were towed over to the Marin Islands, where they lived on the brig and worked the stone quarry (for the private profit of Vallejo's partner, James M. Estell).

There is a San Quentin legend that some of the men on the *Wabau,* not needed for construction work ashore, were "sold" to merchant ships going round the Horn. This seems most unlikely, since the prisoners would have had to be chained to prevent escape, and what sailor could work in irons? It is probably part of the prison mythology.

One thing that is not myth is the presence of at least two women prisoners on the *Wabau* during the two years it took to put up the first building. These ladies, both prostitutes by trade, though in for other offenses, were told to wash and mend the clothes of guards and their fellow convicts, but the most important duties to both women were extracurricular. The guards were not much better or much better off than their charges. They, with their pets among the prisoners, and the girls had a pretty hilarious time of it, with plenty of raw liquor available. But the rank and file of prisoners, working in chains (as they had worked the Angel Island quarry or graded the streets of San Francisco in chains when they were on the *Euphemia*), half starved and in filthy rags, were no better off than were Campbell's slaves on the English hulks half a century before. A committee from the Legislature which inspected them at work delivered themselves of a masterly understatement: "These unfortunate people present a pale and careworn appearance."

6

The first effective prison reforms, starting in England and spreading to the Continent, were largely the work of Quakers, though John Howard himself was not one. This is to be expected: the Society of Friends has always been in the forefront of humanitarian causes and enterprises. As far back as 1682, Penn's "Great Law" for Pennsylvania and West Jersey (later superseded) provided for prisons which were to be "workhouses, free as to fees, food, and lodging," where felons were to "make compensation" by working as "bondsmen." Corporal punishment and the death penalty were both abolished. As Hermann Mannheim well stated, the reintroduction of the English criminal law in these colonies in 1718 was "a backward step."

There were stirrings of prison reform in the air, however, both in England and abroad, before John Howard and Elizabeth Fry. The difference was that those who came before them argued or even investigated, but never implemented their views. Both before and after them, indeed, legislation far outran activation.

It is not strange that so many of the early reformers advocated solitary imprisonment—Dr. Thomas Bray in 1710, for instance, for those under sentence of death; Bishop Joseph Butler in 1740, for all prisoners. The most obvious evil of the eighteenth-century prisons was the utter lack of privacy. To the religiously minded of the time, to whom crime was a matter of free will, there could be no rehabilitation of the criminal except by his own repentance. And how could he ever repent unless he could be alone to meditate? Even Howard agreed to this for a while: he favored "so many small rooms or cabins, that each criminal may sleep alone. . . . Solitude and silence are favorable to reflection, and may possibly lead to repentance." But after he had seen solitary imprisonment at work in Holland and Switzerland he changed his mind and remarked that "absolute solitude . . . is more than human nature can bear without the hazard of distraction or despair." It is unfortunate that a little later the founders of the "Pennsylvania System" did not remember his words. Mrs. Fry opposed solitary confinement for the same reason. The French Revolutionary Penal Code of 1791 ordered prisoners to be confined "alone, with no communication," but this too was a reform measure; it was put on the same terms as the abolition of irons or branding and the necessity of ventilation and light. Joseph II of Austria had already made these same provisions in 1755—though with the addition of a bread-and-water diet. Indeed, the very first mention of solitary cells as a means of repentance (the Church and its Inquisition already had solitary cells, but they were purely for punishment; the unfortunates in them were left to starve to death) was by Jean Mabillon in the 17th century. His recommendation was an almost complete anticipation of the Pennsylvania System: "Penitents might be secluded in cells . . . and there employed in various sorts of labor. To each cell might be joined a little garden, where at appointed hours they might take an airing and cultivate the ground. They might, while assisting in public worship, be placed in separate stalls."

In a sense, the English houses of correction (the first was in London in 1552) and the later European rasp houses constituted a sort of prison reform. Conditions were not much better in them than in the prisons for felons, but at least the prisoners were not idle. Originally the house of correction was intended to be complementary to the workhouse—the former for petty criminals (as in the first Bridewell in 1557), beggars, and vagrants, the latter for orphans and old and infirm paupers. By 1610 only "idle rogues" were sent to a house of correction; the "deserving poor," to a workhouse. Gradually the functions of the two became confused, and today, so far as either still exists, they are merely two names for the same thing. This became especially true in America, where a house of correction might be combined either with an almshouse or a county jail.

On the Continent, the great exemplar was the workhouse in Ghent, already mentioned, established in 1773, and directed by Jacques Philippe Vilain, viscount and burgomeister. This *Maison de Force* had classification by sex and offense, a chaplain and a physician, training in various trades, and individual cells. Vilain, who has been called "the father of penitentiary science," believed that all sentences should be for a year at least, to give time to train the convict in a useful trade, but he was opposed

46

to life sentences. He was a strict disciplinarian but allowed no cruel treatment of prisoners.

The growth of workhouses, where for his own good the prisoner was given productive work to do (Amsterdam had one as early as 1596), came into conflict with public opinion that the thing to do with rogues and paupers was to keep them off the roads and let them languish without competing with free labor. As we have seen, that was at the bottom of the confusion between workhouses and houses of correction. At the other end of the scale was a similar confusion between houses of correction and jails. By 1720 in England many "common prisons" had adjoining houses of correction for minor criminals, who did productive work, whereas felons remained completely idle. On the Continent minor offenders were put into the same prisons as major ones. The keepers of houses of correction began to object. One complained that his institution was "dedicated for sturdy beggars and disobedient children, not for highwaymen and robbers." But the confusion persisted, both in Great Britain and on the Continent. Bavaria in 1751 ruled that "professional thieves and notorious robbers" could be sent to a house of correction for life, "not as punishment but as good discipline." With the increasing use of imprisonment itself as a punishment for crime came a tendency to consider all places of confinement indiscriminately eligible to receive any kind of prisoner.

The *Maison de Force* at Ghent, which was newly built for its purpose, was, incidentally, a pioneer of prison architecture, the first of the octagonal buildings, with cells backed to the inside walls and facing the center. Jeremy Bentham, in his *Panopticon, or the Inspection House,* published in 1789, based his recommendations largely on Ghent, envisaging an octagonal prison with a glass roof to supply light, with cells facing the center and an inspector on duty in the central hall. No prison was ever built exactly according to his specifications, but many nineteenth-century penitentiaries in Europe and South America (including the juvenile reformatory of St. Michael in Rome) approximated it. Its main features became the working model for Auburn in the United States. Auburn's rival, the Cherry Hill prison in Philadelphia, had its cells opening into outdoor exercise yards with their backs to the central portion.

The improvements consequent on early reform legislation were short-lived in most countries; only Holland consistently kept up its standard. Even Joseph II allowed himself to be persuaded to end his very enlightened system of having prisoners work at various industries for pay (half for their present use, half kept for their use after release). He had the machines which he had installed removed, and the whole idea of rehabilitation by work had ended in Austria by 1783. When the French took over Flanders from the Austrians they instituted contract labor, which was a very different thing.

Still, progressive thinkers remained uneasy over prison conditions. In England in 1703 a committee from the Society for Promoting Christian Knowledge investigated Marshalsea and recommended that the inmates should be kept in separate cells—their report was never published until 1849. In 1729 a Parliamentary Committee investigated the Fleet, its chairman being James Oglethorpe, but the only concrete result was that some lightening of overcrowded conditions was effected by sending some of the prisoners to his colony of Georgia. Henry Fielding, who was a justice of the peace as well as a novelist, exposed conditions in the Bridewell in his *Amelia*, but no reforms were instituted in consequence.

In 1764 Cesare Beccaria, in his *Crime and Punishment*, in accordance with his belief that only those crimes that actually endanger society should be considered legal offenses, wrote: "Imprisonment should be more widely employed, but its mode of application should be greatly improved through providing better physical quarters and by separating and classifying the prisoners as to age, sex, and degree of criminality."

In 1773 John Howard was appointed high sheriff of Bedfordshire. His interests hitherto had been largely in science and travel, though he had once been a prisoner of privateers in Brest, and thus had some firsthand experience of what it means to be incarcerated.

He began by inspecting his own county prison, and what he found horrified him. In strong words he spoke of the abuses that "were fitted to cower, snakelike and slimy, in the jungles of darkest barbarism." He perceived instantly that at the base of these abuses lay the system by which jailers subsisted on fees from the prisoners, instead of being salaried. His plea for a change was refused on the grounds of expense to the county. He then toured all the county jails in the hope of finding one which he could use as a precedent; he found none, but he did find conditions as bad as or even worse than in his own Bedfordshire. Thoroughly aroused, he went before a committee of Parliament in 1774 and succeeded in having two ameliorative laws passed. The situation he had disclosed may be judged from the fact that among the improvements ordered were whitewashing of walls and ceilings once a year, cleaning and ventilation of rooms, establishment of medical services and infirmaries, clothing for the near-naked, and "as little use as could be" of underground dungeons.

By this time prison reform had become Howard's chief concern. He announced as his aims "alleviating distress, procuring cleanly and wholesome abodes, exterminating gaol fever, checking impositions and extortions, introduc-

49

ing the habit of industry in Bridewells, restraining shocking debauchery and immorality."

After touring England, Wales, Scotland, and Ireland, he turned his attention to the Continent—at first in the hope that he would find models for English reforms. He did find some, in Amsterdam, Ghent, Rome, and a few other places, but in general the same distressing scenes, with which he had already become familiar at home, presented themselves. In all he made five extensive journeys in the next twelve years, going as far as Russia and Turkey. (The only prison to which he was refused admission was the Bastille in Paris.) After his first extensive trip he published his massive report, *The State of Prisons in England and Wales, with Preliminary Observations . . . and an Account of Some Foreign Prisons.* The first edition came out in 1777; the second, enlarged and revised, in 1789. In 1778 with Sir William Blackstone and Sir William Eden (afterwards Lord Auckland) he drafted the Penitentiary Act, passed the following year. This would have been a great step forward, for it included the abolition of fees, regular inspection, sanitation, and productive work by prisoners. Unfortunately, it cost too much, the public was indifferent, and England was absorbed by its wars with France and America. No prisons were erected, and transportation to Australia was soon substituted.

However, the statement drawn up by this committee put on record the primary aims of early prison reform. The objectives, it said, were "by sobriety, cleanliness, and medical assistance, by a regular series of labour, by solitary confinement during the intervals of work, and by due religious instruction, to preserve and amend the health of the unhappy offenders, to inure them to habits of industry, to guard them from pernicious company, to accustom them to serious reflection, and to teach them both the principles and practice of every Christian and moral duty."

What John Howard wanted for prisoners was security, sanitation, a healthful diet, space to move around in, air to breathe and light to see by, prison officials appointed and paid by public authority, "reasonable work, suitable education, and religious exercises," separation at night but work together during the day without chains or complete enforced silence, and "long sentences with an intention of certain deductions upon their amendment"—in other words, a form of indeterminate sentence. What he actually found, both at home and abroad, is perhaps best evidenced by quoting a few of his findings.

There were several Bridewells in which there was "no allowance of food at all," no work though the prisoners had been committed to hard labor—indeed, no tools or materials with which they *could* work—no water (in the felons' courts of some county jails the inmates were given three pints a day brought in from outside for both drinking and washing), the air so bad that even the leaves of his notebook had to be aired for two hours afterwards. Some had no sewers; those that had, were unkept. There was no bedding, and even straw had to be paid for by the prisoner. In underground dungeons he found one or two inches of water covering the stone floors. Prisoners were kept in irons, and their only recreation was drunkenness or gambling. All new prisoners were ordered to "pay the garnish or strip" (to be beaten).

The improvements Howard suggested indicate still other shortcomings. They included separation of women from men and the young from "old hardened offenders"; paving of the muddy outdoor courts and installation of pumps; provisions for bathing; ovens to destroy vermin; an infirmary with bedding for the sick and cribs for the babies of women prisoners; provision of a grate in the floor for ventilation, which could be closed by a shutter at night, and of hand ventilators in other rooms. There

51

should be a workshop, though felons should not be put to work against their will (in Bridewells, none should be idle but the ill), a chapel with a chaplain, a resident surgeon, and no prisoner should act as a turnkey. No jailer should "hold the tap"—i.e., be licensed to sell liquor. Cleanliness was important: no prison should have within its bounds "a stable, hogcote, or dunghill"—a revelation in itself. "No gaoler should keep more than one dog, and prisoners none." Prisoners should not stay during the day in the rooms in which they slept; they should arise at six o'clock in summer, seven in winter, and start the day with prayers. They should be furnished with bread, and with beef on Sunday, and should receive a penny a day (worth about twenty times that now) to buy "cheese, butter, potatoes, peas, and turnips"—and it should not be the jailer from whom they had to buy them. There should be regular government inspection, and the jailers should receive salaries instead of fees.

In Scotland and Ireland, Howard found nothing to recommend to England, except that in Scotland woman prisoners were not kept in irons. In the Tolbooth in Edinburgh, he reported, "the rich live in comfort and drink whiskey with their visitors, but the poor are closely confined." The house of correction was dirty, and prisoners worked and slept in the same rooms. The Scottish prisons in general had no exercise courts, many had no water or sewers, they were unclean, there was no real separation of the sexes, liquor was sold freely by the keepers, and the prisons were never visited by magistrates.

In Dublin the "new prison" did separate the sexes, but the sickrooms were "too small and not kept clean," the garnish system obtained, and there were dungeons. There were no houses of correction in Ireland, only cages in which the drunk and disorderly were locked up for a night or two. Those acquitted in court still had to stay in prison until they could pay their fees; Howard found boys younger than twelve, almost naked, who had to remain in prison for a year or more for lack of ability to pay a forty-shilling fee.

So much for Britain. Howard went to the Continent with high hopes that he would find better things there. Sometimes he did. The prisons of Holland filled him with admiration: "So quiet, and most of them so clean, that a prisoner can hardly believe to be in a gaol." Each man was in a separate cell, which he never left. Germany and Switzerland were clean, too; in Geneva the sexes were separated, and the food was good. So law-abiding were the Genevans that when he was there the house of correction was empty!

But for the rest, it was a sad story. In Liége he found a curious system: rooms for "dissolute children" consigned to prison by the parents, on the doors of which were such names as Ethiopia, India, Italy, France, and England. Inquiring what this meant, he was told that if the children were inquired after, their respectable families could reply that they were sojourning in whatever country was marked on their cell!

In Hamburg, men, curiously, worked in the spin house, whereas elsewhere it was spin houses for women, rasp houses (shaving wood for dyeing) for men. The Hamburg system was an added punishment, since it was "infamous" for a man to have to do a woman's work.

In Denmark, child-murderers, male or female, were put in the spin house for life, and once a year, on the anniversary of the murder, they were taken to the scene of the crime and whipped. This was considered a great deterrent, since it was dreaded worse than death. In Copenhagen, where the prison was very dirty, prisoners never left their cells, but in warm weather were allowed to open a window. When religious services were held, the doors were opened and the inmates could listen "by an oblique perforation into the church, through a thick wall opposite."

Swedish prisons were even dirtier than the Danish; Howard said he "almost stifled" there. They were dark, and full of "idle people who were drinking." In the city prison in Stockholm, prisoners never left their cells, except that condemned prisoners were taken to the chapel, where a bed was set up for their use; their irons were struck off for the last two days before they died. From the beginning, their coffins had been kept in their cells.

In Russia there were no regular guards, but soldiers were the only keepers. No prisoner ever left his cell except under military guard, and under no conditions were they ever allowed in church. Their only means of subsistence was through voluntary contributions, collected in boxes in the churches and others set up before the gratings of their cells. There was a new penal code, but it introduced no reforms. It did, however, separate accused persons from those convicted, and also separated prisoners to whom imprisonment was their entire punishment, and those to whom it was only a part.

In Venice, Howard found prisoners cast into "loathsome and dark cells for life." In Florence and Milan they were kept in "secrete chambers," but they were not chained, and they had mattresses and good bread. In Rome, in Innocent X's "New Prison" there were strong rooms which were never left except for execution, but there were no irons. In the "prisons at large" there were separate chambers for priests, boys, and "sufferers from cutaneous disorders" (which probably meant syphilis). Here a physician visited the infirmary every morning and came to the very ill in the evening also. Howard admired San Michele (St. Michael) as a prison "for profligate youth, that they who, when idle, were injurious, when instructed ought to be useful to the state." He observed without disapproval the chained boys spinning in silence, watched by guards with whips. In Rome, incidentally, he visited the galleys owned by the Pope, where prisoners were sent for three years or more, chained two by two to the benches; forgers received life sentences, and if they had forged bank notes, they had to wear an iron glove as long as they lived.

In Antwerp he found no prisons, but he did find a cage for torture. In the house of correction in Brussels, one of the prisoners was a former keeper, in for abuse of his trust! As might be expected, Howard was delighted with the Ghent House of Correction and its "well regulated manufactury."

In Portugal, the sexes were separated and garnish was not allowed, but prisoners were detained until they could pay the jailers' fees. In Madrid, also, men and women were separated and women were not chained, but the men lay in irons in dungeon barracks and had to pay if they wanted beds.

Lille, in French Flanders, was dirty and the prisoners suffered from scurvy, but at least the lifers were separated from the short-termers. In Paris, he was pleased to find that the reforms of 1789 had been put into effect; there was separation of the sexes and classification according to age and crime. Prisoners could not be chained except by order of a judge, and infirmaries had been installed. The Conciergerie was clean, with fresh air, the prisoners were allowed to attend mass daily, no garnish was allowed, the soup and bread were good and the inmates received clean linen weekly from a charitable society. Keepers were punished for permitting a prisoner to have hard liquor. Five times a year counselors visited the prison and heard petitions or complaints. But the dark dungeons were "beyond imagination horrid and dreadful." He was not admitted to the Bastille, but he learned quite a bit about it at second hand: the damp and noisome dungeons were infested with rats and toads, the iron chambers were only eight by six feet, with curved ceilings so low a man could not stand upright except in the middle, there were ten-foot-thick walls with only small iron grates for light and air, the prison was freezing in winter and unbearably hot in summer. A former prisoner had established a small library, but few were allowed to use it, and in any case there was not enough light for anyone to read.

Howard's self-appointed mission was to hospitals and lazarettos as well as to prisons and workhouses, and he died a martyr to his cause. In inspecting a military prison at Kherson, in the Ukraine, he contracted "camp fever" (the equivalent of "gaol fever," that is, typhus) from which he died.

Though his work was recognized and praised in England, Howard's influence was greater abroad than at home. It was not so great anywhere as it should have been. For example, in 1814, Prussia issued a series of recommendations exactly paralleling those of Howard's committee in 1778, but with the same lack of practical effect. People took what they wanted of Howard's reforms and ignored his fundamental principles—like H. B. Wagnitz, a Lutheran pastor in Halle who was interested in prison reform. He was for "moral instruction" of prisoners and the establishment of "seminaries" to train prison keepers and guards, but also advocated "scanty food" and hard—i.e., unproductive—labor, to neither of which Howard would have agreed. In 1812, 90 per cent of all English prisons outside county jurisdiction were no better than when Howard had visited and condemned them a half century earlier. (And three-fifths of the prisoners in England were in for debt.)

Nevertheless, John Howard's name shines as the true

pioneer of modern prison reform. His devoted labors opened the way for the early Quaker reformers and their followers.

7

There were people in America also interested in the welfare of prisoners at the same time that John Howard was carrying on his pioneer mission in England and elsewhere. Primarily they were the Quakers. As early as 1776 the Philadelphia Society for the Relief of Distressed Prisoners collected (in wheelbarrows trundled through the city) food and clothing for prisoners. The next year the British occupied Philadelphia, and the society's work came to an end. But in 1787 it was reorganized as the Philadelphia Society for Alleviating the Miseries of Public Prisons and resumed lay visiting and material aid.

It is not known whether Stephen Grellet (Etienne de-Grellet deMobillier) was a member of this society, but early in the nineteenth century he took up the cause of prison reform. He was a French-American Quaker, son of the controller of the Mint in France. In 1812 he went to England to investigate prison conditions there. In that innocent time, he could do so though the two countries were at war.

Joseph Fry and his wife, Elizabeth Gurney Fry, both members of long-time Quaker families of prosperous merchants and bankers, were leading figures among the English Friends. In days when no woman thought of speaking in public, outside of the tolerant Quaker meetings, Mrs. Fry was acknowledged as a minister. Whenever the annual meeting of the Society of Friends was held, the Frys held open house for the visitors from other parts of England. It is natural that Stephen Grellet immediately sought them out. On February 5, 1813, Elizabeth Fry wrote in her diary: "Lately have been seeing after the prisoners in Newgate, with Anna Buxton." (Anna Buxton was her sister-in-law.)

Grellet had already had a glimpse of what Newgate was like and had learned to agree with the writer in the London *Chronicle*, who said that "of all the seats of woe on this side hell, few, I suppose, exceed or equal Newgate." He had started by holding night meetings for "thieves, prostitutes, and pickpockets," at which he tried to find out in what way they could be helped to abandon crime and lead honorable lives. The chief police magistrate offered to "collect all there were" for him, but instead he asked for a permit to visit the prison in which most of them landed for a good part of their lives.

He was permitted to visit Newgate, but was barred from the women's section. There, the officials said, they "could not be responsible; the least that would happen to him would be having his clothes torn off him." He insisted and was admitted at last. What he saw aroused his pity and anger.

Newgate had been burned down in the Gordon Riots in 1780; this was the new building, erected in 1782. It had no windows whatever. Over the doorways, in grisly promise, was carved a design made up of leg irons, fetters, and chains. There were no through drafts. Grellet said "the foulness of the air was almost insupportable." The women slept on the floor or in two tiers of hammocks. The sick were kept upstairs, lying on the bare floor or on a little old straw, with hardly any covering. There were babies born in prison who were stark naked, for their mothers had no way to find clothing for them. Members of both sexes who were ill were tended, so far as they were tended at all, by men. And no matter how ill a prisoner was, he or she still lay in heavy leg irons. Those condemned to death were kept in their nine-by-six-by-nine-foot cells in the old, unburned part of the building even if they were sick or dying. There was no improvement from the seventeenth century when George Fox, the Quaker leader who served terms in six prisons, wrote in his *Journal* of lying on the bare floor "with excrement over my shoes." And none of these wretched, penniless men and women could leave the prison until they had somehow paid the fees they owed the jailer.

Grellet's first practical action was to ask his friends among the Quaker women to sew flannel garments to cover the naked babies, and then to provide some kind of covering for the grown near-naked prisoners. It was to take this clothing and distribute it that Elizabeth Fry and Anna Buxton first entered Newgate.

Mrs. Fry too was warned that she would be in danger of attack if she dared to let herself be surrounded by the vicious, quarrelsome, uncontrolled mob of criminal women. She paid no attention to the warning. From the beginning the miserable creatures felt instinctively that she was their friend. (As the Reverend C. B. Taylor put it, "She never said 'you,' but 'us.' ") Busy as she was with her home, her large family of children, and her many duties as a Quaker minister, she resolved to do something to help. What she did in the remaining thirty-two years of her life made her known as "The Angel of Newgate."

Though she devoted herself largely to the female inmates, her interest always extended to all prisoners. Howard's prime motive had been the reform of the prisons and the prison systems themselves; Mrs. Fry's was directed toward the inmates as redeemable human beings. Her four principles were that there must be religious instruction, classification of prisoners by sex, age, and offense, employment instead of corroding idleness—employment that

59

would bring some profit to the workers—and that only woman officers should ever be in charge of woman prisoners.

She began by going regularly to read to the women in Newgate, most of whom were utterly illiterate. They were quiet, and they listened. Then she proposed starting a school to teach reading, writing, and arithmetic to the utterly neglected children—children of prisoners, or prisoners themselves. The authorities would not give her a room, so the women crowded themselves together even more than they had been crowded before, to make space for the school. Its first teacher was an educated woman who was in for stealing a watch! Then the women wanted to learn too and begged for a chance.

A meeting was held in the Fry home with the governor and ordinary (chaplain) of the prison and two sheriffs, then another in the prison with the officers and inmates together. Mrs. Fry formed the women into an Association, and they cooperated enthusiastically. With her husband's help, she organized the Ladies' Newgate Committee, to raise money for materials and to give a small salary to a full-time matron. The prisoners were to be taught to read and write and sew, and they were to make articles to sell. A disused laundry was fitted out as a schoolroom. The first class consisted of seventy women, one third of them totally illiterate, another third who could read a little. All, she said "ought to be taught to read, write, and cipher, as well as make a ready and profitable use of the needle."

The school was run democratically, the women helping to make their own rules. There were rewards for good conduct, but no punishments except exile from the school, which was run on the Lancastrian method, with literate prisoners as monitors.

Within a month, what had justly been called "hell on earth" had been transformed into "the appearance of

an industrious manufactury or a well-regulated family."
While the women sewed somebody read aloud to them
from entertaining as well as pious books. Each wore a
blue apron, with a numbered ticket tied around her neck
with red tape.

Mrs. Fry had been warned against competition with free
labor, and she worked early for what is now known as
"state use"—manufacture of articles for use by public institutions. Meanwhile a little shop was opened like the
craft or hobby shop of a modern prison. The women
knitted stockings, and made many patchwork quilts, which
were extremely popular among the convicts who had been
transported to Botany Bay. Members of the Association
pledged themselves not to drink, and not to beg from
visitors as they had done previously. They had no need
now to beg, though they earned less than the then going
wage of eighteen pence a week for such work. Most of the
money was kept for the day of transportation or release,
but some of it was spent for tea and sugar.

So amazed and encouraged were the authorities that before long they adopted Mrs. Fry's system as part of the
regular regimen of Newgate, and they paid part of the
matron's salary in exchange for permission to punish recalcitrant women by short terms of confinement. The
Grand Jury of the City of London in 1818 not only approved the plan but suggested that it be applied to men
as well, "as a means of converting a prison into a school
of reform."

There was some opposition, even among the Quakers
themselves, but Elizabeth Fry persisted in her humanitarian mission. She was the first woman not a queen to
appear before the House of Commons. There she pleaded
for woman wardens, in a separate prison for women; for
state-use labor "at fair rates"; for classification and separation, especially at night; against solitary imprisonment

"except in very atrocious cases." She got none of these at once, but the ball had started rolling. Interest was aroused not only throughout England, but abroad.

Her approach to the prisoners was always woman to woman, human being to human being. Until her last illness, in 1843, she visited every convict ship carrying women to Australia, and she succeeded in having separate quarters for them, freeing them from chains, having a school for children on each ship for the eight months' voyage, and changing the rules so that no woman could be deported until she had weaned her youngest child, and that women could take with them to Botany Bay all their children under the age of seven.

Though there were murmurs from the Friends' Meeting, from 1818 on Mrs. Fry traveled widely to observe prison conditions and preach her gospel of prisoners' self-help. Her work had already begun to bear fruit. In 1816 her two brothers-in-law, Sir Thomas Fowell Buxton and Samuel Hoare, were prominent in the formation of the Society for the Reformation of Prison Discipline. She herself formed the Ladies' Prison Committee, which made gifts of needed articles to woman prisoners and started libraries in all prisons—with the proviso that they should contain "no novels, plays, and other improper books." (The Ladies' Committee is now the British Society of Ladies, with the Duchess of Gloucester as its patroness.)

Mrs. Fry's first trip was to the north of England and Scotland, with her brother, Joseph Gurney. In 1821, with her husband and daughters, she visited prisons in eleven English towns. In later trips she went to Ireland, France, Belgium, Holland, Switzerland, Germany, and Denmark. At the same time she carried on an increasingly large correspondence with interested persons from all over Europe. Her influence with governmental authorities was great, and her constant effort was to legalize the reforms that had thus far been made only on a voluntary and unenforceable basis.

In 1827 she published her *Observations on the Visiting, Superintendance, and Government of Female Prisoners.* Committees similar to the one she had founded sprang up all over the Continent, though few of their members possessed her quick fellow-feeling and her sound common sense. However, there were some quite concrete results. In 1840 she had the pleasure of visiting Theodor Fliedner, in Kaiserswerth, who directly from her inspiration had founded the Rhenish-Westphalian Prison Association, which did nursing in prisons and provided a refuge for discharged prisoners with nowhere to go.

Byron might jeer at Mrs. Fry in *Don Juan,* but most of England revered her. She spent herself unceasingly in the cause. Her last efforts were to relieve the harshness of treatment of inmates of the new Pentonville prison, but by this time she was too old and too ill to do much in person. Still, she took an active part in a meeting of the Ladies' Society only three months before she died, at sixty-five years of age, in 1845. Perhaps her best epitaph and the keynote of all her work was uttered by Lord Ashley when he said, "She respected human nature."

Prison reform in England was now in full flood. Besides Buxton and Hoare (and others of the Gurney and Fry families), the chief protagonists in this period were Jeremy Bentham, Sir Samuel Romilly, and Sir James Mackintosh. These men not only helped reform English criminal law (greatly reducing the number of capital offenses), but they also had a great deal to do with the establishment of the new prisons for felons—originally a reform measure, however bad they may seem in the light of modern penology.

But by this time they were reflecting American originals. The American penitentiary in both its forms—Cherry

63

Hill and Auburn—is the father of the nineteenth-century prison everywhere. Alas, it has been remarked that Elizabeth Fry, in her devoted efforts to make things better for prisoners, inadvertently succeeded only in making them worse!

8

"The prison as we know it," say Barnes and Teeters, "was given to the world by America." Jefferson, as long ago as 1788, drew plans for a prison one of whose features was to be solitary confinement. Jails, workhouses, and houses of correction came from England, but the penitentiary is a peculiarly American phenomenon, though affected by Beccaria, Howard, and Bentham.

The first American prisons were known as penitentiaries (originally a place in which one might achieve penitence, or what we should call a reformatory), and wherever you find so-called felony prisons, there is the American influence. Today "penitentiary" is merely an alternative term for a maximum security prison, though sometimes the word has been used to denote a prison, incarceration in which is a substitute for capital punishment.

The earliest solitary penitentiary in the world built specifically for that purpose was Cherry Hill, in Philadelphia. It was preceded by the old Walnut Street jail, the nature of whose early control and discipline is evidenced by the fact that the first time a clergyman ventured to preach to the inmates in the prison yard, the warden posted a cannon and a man with a lighted match, all ready to fire to protect him if it became necessary. (It was not necessary.)

"The Quakers," as Frederick H. Wines says, "took up the cause of prison reform and made a religion of it." Unfortunately, their own religion was one of silent meditation and soul-searching, and they made the fundamental mistake of assuming that ordinary worldly lawbreakers would be amenable to the same discipline. Their primary aim was to provide a place where prisoners would be well fed and clothed, and given sufficient air, light, and exercise, but with each individual kept strictly apart from all others, so that he might reflect on his crimes and duly repent of them and thus return to society as a well-adjusted, honest man. At least one important and beneficent feature of Cherry Hill was that every inmate capable of work was kept occupied during all his waking hours. Later imitations of its system omitted even this provision: the Western Pennsylvania Penitentiary, in Pittsburgh, deliberately kept all its inmates idle for a number of years.

Before Cherry Hill (its official title was the Eastern Penitentiary of Pennsylvania) was opened in 1829, attempts at reformation had already been made at the turbulent Walnut Street jail. There was some classification of prisoners. Those who wished to work were furnished the means of productive labor for which they were paid, and there was even a rough attempt at partial self-government (presumably after the episode of the clergyman and the cannon!). From 1795–1799 the jail even had a woman warden, Mrs. Mary Weed, whose husband had died of yellow fever in office, and who was appointed to succeed him. She is probably the only woman warden of a men's prison in history.

In a sense, indeed, the Walnut Street jail (which was purely a city prison) may be considered the pioneer of the so-called Pennsylvania system. As early as 1757 the famous Dr. Benjamin Rush had advocated classification of prisoners, separation of debtors from felons, and a sort of indeterminate sentence, whereby a man could earn remission of part of his sentence by hard labor and good behavior. In 1790 a block of cells was erected in the yard of the jail for the "more hardened offenders." This was known as the "penitentiary house," the first use of this name on record.

The full-fledged inception of the system of solitary imprisonment with full employment did not come, however, until the opening of the Cherry Hill penitentiary in 1829, when its rival, the Auburn system (which will be considered later) was already in operation.

Cherry Hill was built and operated with just one idea in mind—to make it a model to the world. The building was circular, with all the cells opening outward, each into its small walled exercise yard. The prisoner in each cell worked, ate, and slept in it, and took his exercise alone in his own yard. He saw no other human being except prison officers and official visitors from outside, including clergymen; one or another of these visited him frequently and regularly, talked to him to find out his "state of mind" and to exhort him to better things, and left him reading matter. He was brought into the prison blindfolded, and throughout his term—which might mean for the rest of his life, for there were many lifers—he never saw either the rest of the prison or any of his fellow inmates.

The cells were fairly large, for they were workshops as well. Only work that could be done by a man alone and in a cell could be carried on. This included such handicrafts as spinning, weaving, dyeing, and shoemaking. The work was all done for private industries, and the profit went to upkeep of the prison.

It must never be forgotten that this solitary system, which seems so cruel to us, was instituted solely as a means of reformation, by high-minded, humanitarian reformers. When what became known as the Pennsylvania system was first broached, Zephaniah Swift said: "The world has never before witnessed such an example of benevolence

66

in the mode of punishing criminals." But under it men went mad, or deteriorated mentally to imbecility, or died because they no longer had the will to live. Man is a gregarious animal, and only the exceptional, with unusual inner resources, can long endure the terrors of isolation. The prisoners at Cherry Hill had the alleviation of their official visitors, but these did not provide companionship in any true meaning of the term.

Most visitors to Cherry Hill were loud in its praises. The exception was Charles Dickens, who in his youth, as the child of an imprisoned debtor, had known all the horrors of the promiscuous English prison and was vitally interested in penal reform. He investigated Cherry Hill hopefully during his first lecture tour in America, only to conclude: "In its intention, I am well convinced that it is kind, humane, and meant for reformation: but . . . very few men are capable of estimating the immense amount of torture and agony which this dreadful punishment, prolonged for years, inflicts upon the sufferers."

The alternative to the Pennsylvania system was the Auburn or Congregate system. It took its name from the establishment of Auburn Penitentiary in New York, in 1816, followed in 1825 by Sing Sing. It really antedated the Pennsylvania system, and it too was the work of sincere reformers.

By the Auburn system, prisoners worked together in large workshops, but slept and spent all out-of-work hours in solitary cells. When they were together during the day, they had to preserve utter silence under penalty of flogging. They took their exercise together, but in silence. Even the appearance of communication between prisoners was punished severely. In going to or from cells, or during exercise, the men had to face the officer in charge, or else look downwards, each man with his hand on the shoulder of the man in front. It was probably at Auburn that daring prisoners first learned to speak in low tones out of the corner of the mouth, a characteristic which, with the shuffling step and the prison pallor, for many years was the sure sign that a man had "done time."

Auburn and the prisons that followed it were built with inside cells, back to back, seven-by-seven by three-and-a-half feet—really a shell of cell blocks inside the buildings, facing inward, with barred doors. They were damp in summer, icy in winter, with the only light and air coming from small, heavily barred niches in the high outside wall.

Though these prisons were intended to be corrective of the evils of the old-time squalid, turbulent institutions of both England and America, they rapidly became places of horror, based on the theory that "hard work can both punish and regenerate" and that the way to force the prisoner to do hard work was by a liberal use of the wire cat-o'-nine-tails. In Auburn and Sing Sing, of which he was the first warden, the guiding spirit behind this hard-boiled attitude was Elam Lynde. Lynde's conviction was that all convicts were cowards, and that the only way to run a prison was to break the prisoner's spirit. Inmates were flogged for every error, without discrimination—even the epileptic and the insane—up to five hundred strokes on occasion. Lynde's remedy for every breach of discipline was "instant flogging."

From 1821–1823, Auburn tried out the Pennsylvania system in eighty cells, but so many of the prisoners responded with broken health or broken minds that this experiment was abandoned. Sing Sing was deliberately built on the principle that "to make any impression upon convicts there must be suffering, and to make any adequate impression, such suffering as will excite feelings of terror."

Other state prisons, as they were established, copied, for the most part, the Auburn system and went it one better if that were possible. In Massachusetts it was felt that the prisoner's mind must be "reduced to a state of humiliation. . . . The punishment of the convict is incomplete, so long as his mind is not conquered." Until 1829, the prisoner's arm was tattooed with the name of the institution, so that after his release he would never be able to hide the fact that he was an ex-convict.

This was the system, complete with dungeons and irons for insubordinates, which won the day in America and even today still exists in some parts of the world. The Pennsylvania system, based on belief in free will and the value of introspection, was tried out for periods up to twenty-nine years in New Jersey, Maryland, Maine, Rhode Island, and Massachusetts, only to be abandoned. Actually only the two Pennsylvania penitentiaries and New Jersey ever tried it in full detail, as the early Philadelphia reformers had envisaged it. The conflict between the two systems did not end officially until 1913, when the Eastern Pennsylvania Penitentiary was transformed into a congregate prison. By 1869, Western Pennsylvania had rejected the system, and in Philadelphia it had long been abandoned in all but name. Only the cost of remodeling prison buildings slowed up the change.

In Europe, South America, and elsewhere its fate was different. Even today many European and South American prisons are still conducted on the solitary system. For this, the worst feature, overrode all the excellent reforms which had made the Walnut Street prison and then Cherry Hill the cynosure of prison reformers from all over the world.

The victory of the Auburn system was partly due to the inhumanity of solitary confinement, its injury to health, sight, and mind, but basically it was economic. It was, as Louis N. Robinson has remarked, "more profitable to turn prisons into factories." In Europe, where, in general, prisoners were kept idle, it was a better means to discipline than allowing convicts to mingle. But in America, say Sheldon and Eleanor Glueck, the chief aim of a prison became "to manufacture articles rather than to remake human beings." This was especially true until, after the reforms of the turn of the century, work for state use became the usual thing; states (and individuals) could grow rich on the unpaid labor of convicts for private contractors or employers.

Gradually all the states, except Delaware, ceased housing prisoners in local jails and built their own state prisons. (The Federal government to this day puts some of its nonmilitary short-termers and even some long-termers in state institutions.) Connecticut's was the first, built for prisoners who under an earlier law would have been executed. Virginia followed, then Massachusetts.

In the dog-eat-dog world of the burgeoning industrial system, any idea of reform aimed at rehabilitation was forgotten. Prisoners were practically slaves, and the harsher their treatment the better. America never reverted to the "hell on earth" of the eighteenth-century prison (except in county and city jails, of which more later), but it created a fine "hell on earth" of its own. Conditions in some state prisons in the mid-nineteenth century made Auburn seem a paradise. One example was California, in the early days of San Quentin and Folsom. Not only was San Quentin at this period (despite sporadic attempts at reform by an occasional farsighted warden) wide open to corruption, bribery, and scandal, and insufferably overcrowded from its beginning, but the methods of discipline and punishment were cruel almost beyond belief.

In an attempt to ameliorate the system of constant and excessive flogging, fourteen dungeon cells, eleven-and-a-half by six feet, were added to the first building. In them the men under punishment were chained to iron rings

70

embedded in the stone walls and left there often for years, without bedding or toilet facilities, on a starvation diet, in the dark; when they were released half their heads were shaved to distinguish them. As Kenneth Lamott has observed, the prison directors, "high-minded men with the best of intentions, put into use the dungeon which was to remain the shame of San Quentin for eighty years." Whipping still went on, at a post called the "ladder," which was really a cross: in England men were bared to the waist for whipping, to protect the groin; in San Quentin they were lashed stark naked. Another punishment was the "shower bath," a hard stream from a one-and-a-half-inch hose until "blood bursts from the eyes and ears, and syncope intervenes." The ladder was abolished in 1880; the shower bath, in 1882.

But they were followed by other tortures in the name of punishment. Folsom had the "derrick," which was a block and tackle from which men hung for five hours at a time, with only the tips of their toes on the floor. The floor itself was spread with chloride of lime, whose fumes arose to burn and suffocate them. In San Quentin an "incorrigibles department" was opened, where disturbers—and also the "disturbed"—were held in sheet-iron cells, six by four feet. Folsom introduced in 1884, and San Quentin in 1900, punishment by the straitjacket, a canvas four feet long, which was so tightly cinched that the lacings cut into the flesh; the man was gagged (one man died of suffocation in consequence) and then kicked, beaten, and bounced around like a ball at the pleasure of the guards. The record for endurance in this canvas coffin was 139 hours! Men came out of it with ruined kidneys and damaged hearts, to say nothing of its mental effect.

This, together with bad and scanty food, conspicuous stripes or other humiliating uniforms, primitive sanitation, and little or no attempt at religious, educational, or medical care, was the average American prison throughout most of the nineteenth century.

Abroad, where the American idea of the penitentiary, in one or the other of its two forms, had caught like wildfire, conditions were, if anything, worse.

<h1 style="text-align:center">9</h1>

The next turning point in penology, which gradually led from the degeneration of both the Pennsylvania and Auburn systems to a new flood tide in prison reform, began in the United States after the Civil War. But before and beyond then, the idea of the penitentiary—mostly with its harsher features retained and its more progressive ones ignored—had had major repercussions both in Great Britain and Ireland and on the Continent.

In England itself it led to the establishment of a number of new prisons, which in time ended the need for the hulks and finally brought an end to transportation. Milbank, in 1816, was the first of these. It was intended to be built on the principles laid down by Bentham in his *Panopticon*—an octagon-shaped building on the Auburn plan, with all cells facing inwards and armed guards in the central portion—but in the end it was modified a good deal from Bentham's specifications.

Parkhurst, for juvenile offenders, followed in 1839, and Pentonville, which was announced as the model for all future prison buildings, in 1842, then Portland in 1849 and Dartmoor in 1850. The first English National Penitentiary, Milbank, in hexagon (not octagon) form, with its six cell blocks, each adjacent to one side of a hexagon-shaped center, was designed for all felons not transported or sentenced to the hulks. The first six months in this prison—and varying periods in all English prisons—had to be spent in solitary, so that it was really a combination of the two American systems. The first county jail according to the "new system" was at Reading, in 1845—the jail in which Oscar Wilde was confined.

The difficulty was that up to 1877 England had two separate prison administrations, local and national. Peel's Gaol Act of 1823 was the first real reform, but it could cover only prisons under county jurisdiction, with no national administrative control. The conditions in county and municipal prisons (jails) can be gathered from the fact that the Act provided that if a prisoner could not be given a separate cell, he must at least have a bed to himself!

The 1823 Act was a great improvement, but it had its defects. One was that it was vague as to methods of classification, and in consequence the young and old, the petty offender and the habitual criminal, were still in many cases housed in common rooms and dormitories. In reaction, solitary came more and more to be applied. (This was directly opposed to Elizabeth Fry's plan of segregation.) Flogging continued to be the common means of discipline. Prisoners of the first class, sentenced to hard labor, had to put in their first three months at the treadmill, stonebreaking and similar forms of made work. Only women and those under sixteen were exempted.

That the Act had failed to eradicate the appalling conditions in local prisons is shown by the fact that the Grand Jury of Middlesex in 1824 condemned Newgate as a public nuisance. Newgate, however, continued as it was. In 1835 the office of prison inspectors was created. Three years later came a strong recommendation from the authorities that separate confinement be the preferred method, on the model of the Pennsylvania system; however, the complete solitude of Cherry Hill was never resorted to in English prisons. By the Prison Act of 1865, separation was ordered for the first nine months, with six

73

more months added if the convict's behavior had been bad. In Pentonville it was two years before an inmate could mingle with his fellows, plus a year and a half more for misbehavior. In general, some such provision still obtains in English prisons. First offenders are known as "star prisoners," and have a shorter time of preliminary solitary confinement.

There were, however, some excellent points in the first reform ordinance in 1823. Even in solitary the prisoner had daily visits from the chaplain, the surgeon, and a keeper, and once a month one from a visiting magistrate.

Though, as has been said, the national government did not have control over local prisons until 1877, they were, by 1850, subject to approval by the Secretary of State. The first surveyor-general of prisons, appointed in 1844, was Sir Joshua Jebb, who had built Pentonville.

Not all the reforms in English prisons came from American influence. Much of the improvement during the nineteenth century was a direct reflection of Sir Walter Crofton's reforms in Ireland, and Crofton, in turn, had learned from Captain Alexander Maconochie, in Australia.

Maconochie in 1840 was appointed governor of Norfolk Island, 800 miles off the coast of Australia, to which island the "twice condemned"—those who had committed fresh crimes after they were transported—were consigned. Before his administration, Norfolk Island can be described only as pure hell. The gallows was never taken down; it was needed constantly. The men worked, ate, and slept in heavy irons. The slightest sign of resentment or a word of contradiction or lack of sufficient subservience to even a private soldier was accounted as "insolence" and punished by flogging with the cat, gagging, or solitary confinement on bread and water. When a Roman Catholic priest, Father Ullathorne, went there in 1834 to give the last rites to convicts condemned to death for an abortive re-

74

bellion, those who were to die fell on their knees and thanked God, while the men who had been reprieved burst into sobs and tears.

Maconochie changed all this speedily by institution of what he called his correctional apparatus, the mark system. It was a form of indeterminate sentence. As he said, "When a man keeps the key of his own prison, he is soon persuaded to fit it to the lock." For "time sentences" he substituted "task sentences." A man had so many "marks" to earn; when he had earned them he had earned commutation of his sentence as well. Marks were given not only for work accomplished but also for good behavior, "frugality of living," and acquisition of "habits of industry." "While in prison he should earn everything he receives; all sustenance and indulgences should be added to his debt of marks." After a man had earned the right, he became one of a small group working together, and the group as a whole was responsible for the conduct of every member. As the end of a prisoner's time approached, he was put under easier discipline as a preparation for his return to society.

Alas, Maconochie was in advance of his time, and after too short a period he was recalled. Norfolk Island lapsed into the bad old days. But news of his accomplishment had spread, and in 1853 Crofton, who was chairman of the Board of Directors for Convict Prisons in Ireland, introduced the mark system in his jurisdiction.

There were four steps in Crofton's adaptation of the "apparatus." A prisoner first spent nine months in solitary in Mountjoy Prison, near Dublin, picking oakum. Then he was sent to Spike Island, in the Cove of Cork, where he was set to public works. There he entered the lowest of five classes, rising from each to the next by his industry and good conduct, or falling back into a lower one by reason of the lack of these qualities. When he had earned sufficient marks to be "graduated" from the top class, he was transferred to an institution at either Lusk or Smithfield. These were open prisons, "a filter between the prison and the community," where the men worked on their own, without supervision, returning to the prison after work. At the same time there were evening technical classes in various trades. The only punishment, as before, was to be recommitted to a lower category. Finally the prisoner was released, but it was a conditional release, like parole, with supervision and reports for a year. There were 720 marks from solitary to the first grade, then 2920 a year in each succeeding grade up to his release.

The Irish system was very widely copied, in England not less than on the Continent. In England it was chiefly applied to juveniles, and in the end led to the Borstal plan, which will be mentioned later. Most English prisons, however, continued for most of the century in the sort of treatment and discipline established at Pentonville and Milbank. They varied both in severity—at Wormwood Scrubs, for instance, there was emphasis on "made" hard labor: the crank, the treadmill, shot drill, and stonebreaking, though all the prisons had this to a certain extent— and in the nature of the work prisoners were ordered to do. By the progressive stage system a man might be transferred from one prison to another by reason of his good or bad conduct. There were three "public works" prisons: the making of a breakwater at Portland, on the coast of Dorsetshire; work on the docks in Chatham; and land reclamation at Dartmoor.

As Hugh Klare, secretary of the Howard League for Prison Reform, has said: "The nineteenth-century answer [in England] to prison hulks was the erection of specially built permanent gaols. . . . [with] punitive repression, strict separation, silence, the discipline of the treadmill." All one can say is that they were better than the degradation of the eighteenth-century jail or the early hulks.

The concern for some reform of penal institutions spread throughout the British Empire, even to British India. The one place where it lagged behind seemed to be Canada, then largely an undeveloped country. (Canada did not become a federal union until 1867, when the Dominion government took over the Provincial prisons.) A survey of Canadian prisons made at this time showed deplorable conditions. Rockhead Prison, in Halifax, was found to be "filthy"; the prisoners "ordered the guards around," addressing them by their given names; the schoolmaster was "indolent"; meals in the dining room were a continuous "rough-house." At St. John, New Brunswick, where at least the men were not idle, but manufactured tubs, brooms, and clothespins, there was no school at all, and no library, and the chaplain, unless sent for, appeared only on Sundays. At Kingston, Ontario, the oldest Canadian prison, founded in 1835, there were no sewers and no baths; typhoid fever and constant diarrhea were common. There was no heat, and the convicts had to sleep in all their clothes during winter to keep out the cold. There was no discipline except by flogging.

Today, as we shall see, Canada is keeping pace with modern prison conditions and the treatment of prisoners.

On the Continent the general interest in that American institution, the penitentiary, and later in the English and Irish reforms, had wide if sporadic effects. For the most part, in the countries of western and central Europe, the principle was to provide prisoners with the bare essentials of food and clothing, and to require them to earn anything more than this by their "exertion . . . a strong incitement to the formation of habits of industry."

Crofton's system especially was copied more or less in France, Italy, Holland, Germany, Hungary, Denmark, Norway, and Switzerland. In Saxony, Eugéne d'Aligne established three "progressive disciplinary classes," for "reformation by individualization."

G. M. Obermaier, who was first head of the Kaiserslauten and then of the Munich prison from 1830–1852, had all corporal punishment stopped, ended the use of bloodhounds to keep prisoners in order, and allowed only guards outside the prison grounds to be armed. He established libraries in both prisons, and started an hour's schooling every day. The convicts worked in textile manufacture under state control and received current wages, with a third taken off for their maintenance. The Bavarian Crime Code of 1813 had already established minimum and maximum (indeterminate) sentences, facilitating Obermaier's reforms.

In Spain Colonel Manuel Montesinos, director of the Valencia prison in 1835, and at a later period *visitador* (inspector) of the General Spanish Prisons, was inspired by Crofton's example to institute a system by which a prisoner could earn up to half the time off on his sentence. "The moral object of penal establishments," he said, "should be not so much to inflict punishment as to correct, to receive men idle and ill-intentioned, and return them to society, if possible, honest and industrious citizens." He formed the prisoners into quasi-military companies, with convicts themselves acting as petty officers, and they organized their own workshops, mostly for textile manufacture. Every prisoner under twenty had to attend school one hour a day. The system was an enormous success, and the morale of the prison soared. But a new code was passed, forbidding the possibility of a man's earning a remission of his sentence. The whole reform plan promptly collapsed, and Montesinos resigned in despair.

In general, throughout Europe, the changes were made not so much for reform or rehabilitation of the prisoner as for easier discipline. The idea of the strict penitentiary, with hard labor and solitary imprisonment, was what attracted the official mind. In 1840 Sweden, for example, took over the Pennsylvania system in its entirety. It was not until 1918 that the period of absolute solitary confinement was cut to the first six months of the sentence, and to three months for minors. The first "new system" prison in Prussia was Rawitsch, built in 1810, which was organized along military lines. A token attempt was made at classification, in that prisoners were divided officially into two categories, but as they were together day and night this had no practical effect. Friedrich Wilhelm IV, an admirer of Elizabeth Fry's, ordered Moabit prison, in Berlin, to be built along the lines of England's pioneer Pentonville, and in 1857 appointed Johann Wichern to reorganize its administration as a social service. But as late as 1924, Prussia still did not have enough prisons with enough cells to permit any real separation between different classifications. In the same way, attempts in other German states to copy Bavaria's indeterminate sentence law failed because there were no "reformative prisons" in which to carry them out.

Belgium also tried "re-education by labor," but it failed because private industry fought against the competition.

What did spread like wildfire over the Continent was the cellular system, usually in close imitation of Cherry Hill. Belgium went the farthest. The prisoners wore masks whenever they had to pass their fellows; they were known strictly by number, never by name. They took their exercise in single yards and sat in chapel in single stalls. (To some reformers, this was not cruelty, but an honorable effort to conceal the identity of the convicts and to protect their families from disgrace.) In 1830 Edouard Ducpetieux, who had once been a political prisoner himself, became the General Inspector of Prisons, and it was he who inaugurated the rigid solitary cell system, which lasted in Belgium until 1919.

It was the same story all over Europe: Baden became the model for all Germany in 1851, with a year to be served in isolated cells (though Dreibergen and Mechlenburg had already anticipated it). The German Criminal Code of 1871 limited isolation to three years—"without the prisoner's consent"! In Holland half the sentence had to be served in solitary; later this was limited to five years. Tuscany, Switzerland, Norway, and Denmark followed suit. The first International Prison Congress, held in Frankfurt in 1846, voted in favor of the cell system, with solitary understood as an inherent part of it. These, however, were advanced reformers, who undoubtedly considered it superior (as it was) to the degraded prisons of the past. Only France, though it made some early gestures, abandoned the cell system, under the Second Empire, in favor of transportation, and from 1853 until 1875 the use of separate cells was either limited or altogether prohibited.

10

In addition to the idea of the penitentiary, either according to the Pennsylvania system or the Auburn system, there was still another American innovation which caught on all over the civilized world. It began a little later than the period of which we have been talking, but it must be described before we can consider the first ripples of the next wave of prison reform. This was the reformatory for young offenders, signalized by the opening of the Elmira, New York, Reformatory in 1876.

Juvenile delinquency is no new problem in America or anywhere else. There have always been "disturbed" boys and girls, even children. The difference is that in the old days a child or adolescent who broke a law was treated exactly like an adult, given the same punishment even to execution or mutilation. We have already seen that children as young as six years of age were incarcerated in the eighteenth-century prisons or hulks.

From the beginning of prison reform this situation troubled the minds and hearts of the reformers. San Michele (the Hospice of St. Michael), in Rome, came into being because of Pope Clement XI's desire to rehabilitate the delinquent young. Since it was a true and harsh prison of its time, it is unlikely that it restored many boys to respectable living. There were other early attempts to provide separate institutions for children and youths, some of which have already been noted.

New York City's House of Refuge for those of both sexes under twenty was founded in 1825, but there were similar institutions in Europe before that date. Philadelphia followed in 1828 and Boston in 1830, but there were only eight such prisons for young delinquents in all America in 1850. By 1921 there were more than a hundred houses of refuge or reformatories for the young in the United States, mostly state institutions.

But the real reformatory idea—that is, an intermediate or minimum security prison designed exclusively for young offenders and embodying the enlightened recommendations of the famous "Cincinnati Declaration" at the first meeting of the American Prison Association in 1870 —was realized, at least partially, with the opening of Elmira Reformatory in 1877, with Z. R. Brockway as its first superintendent. From it grew directly the fine Borstal system in England, which, as Barnes and Teeters remark, is recognized "as far surpassing anything we have here for that purpose." It rose from a visit to Elmira in 1894 by

81

the then director of English prisons. (But even Borstal is not always successful—at least according to Brendan Behan!)

The thirty-seven paragraphs of the Cincinnati Declaration included practically all the points of a modern penal system aimed at reformation instead of punishment, foremost among them progressive classification (the mark system), the indeterminate sentence, and "cultivation of the inmate's self-respect." As another example of the mutual interseeding of ideas, this in turn stemmed from a visit made by Gaylord Hubbell, then warden of Sing Sing, to Ireland in 1863. In other words, it was an outgrowth of the Crofton plan, which was derived from Maconochie. But the New York Legislature refused to consider such a fundamental change in its penal code, and its utmost concession was an agreement to try out the new methods in an institution for young first offenders. Even so, it was eight years more, because of difficulties in financing the project through taxation, before Elmira actually opened its doors.

And even at that, it stretched its age limits beyond what most people would consider a reasonable age, since it took in male offenders from sixteen to thirty. Most of the American reformatories built on its model followed suit, and some even included men up to forty. Until 1900, New York was the only state which had a reformatory for women, though now in most states women, even felons, are usually sent to separate reformatories instead of to state prisons. (In California even a woman condemned to death is kept in the Corona State Institution for Women before she is brought to the gas chamber in San Quentin.)

The early American houses of refuge, which were usually for boys sentenced to serve throughout their minority, already had some anticipations of the methods of treatment which flowered in Elmira; they all had schools, religious care, and some slight form of self-government, though only Boston had organized recreation. Elmira had all these things and more—a library, a prison paper, a gymnasium, an athletic field, a band, a glee club, and much else. The important distinction, however, was the fundamental system of classification, accompanied by the indeterminate sentence.

Elmira inmates were divided into four classes originally, later changed to three. On entrance, they were placed in the middle class, and thereafter they moved up or down, according to their behavior. After six months in the first (highest) grade, an inmate who had reached this classification by earning the necessary marks could be released on parole. (Some sort of parole or ticket-of-leave system has existed in the United States since about 1840.)

Brockway, one of the most advanced penologists of his time, outlined in detail his objectives in Elmira. He wanted cleanliness and sanitation, with plenty of both natural and artificial light. The inmates were to wear no "degradingly distinctive" clothing (i.e., stripes, broad arrows, etc.) but were to be dressed in smart semimilitary uniforms, and they were to keep themselves clean and well groomed. Food was to be plentiful and good.

There were to be classes in academic subjects from kindergarten (rather a remarkable statement!) to the end of high school, with special classes also in college subjects. Thirty-five or more trades were to be taught in vocational classes, besides training in mechanical and freehand drawing, cabinet-making and other wood and metal work, clay modeling, and "cardboard construction" (perhaps *papier maché* work, then very popular): unfortunately there were facilities for only about a third of the inmates in this manual training, which would engage the interest of most boys and young men. The weekly paper was edited and printed by the inmates but was subject to official censorship.

Brockway gave a great deal of thought to rehabilitative recreation. There must be, he said, "no vaudeville or minstrel shows," but plenty of "entertainments such as the middle-cultured people of a community would enjoy." Religious services were to be "adapted to the hereditary, habitual, and preferable denominational predilection of the individual prisoners." Also, he arranged a unique sort of occasion, not primarily educational, recreational, or religious, which he described as "definitely planned, carefully directed, emotional occasions, . . . figuratively, for a kind of irrigation." Exactly of what these consisted is not known; possibly they were patriotic rallies, or some sort of lectures or discussions or concerts.

Elmira was organized rather on the model of a first-class military school; there was a "regimental military organization" with drill and marching to the music of the band, swords for the officers and dummy guns for the privates. But the important thing was not any of these extraneous matters, but the basic system of earning one's way out. After an inmate had made his way up from the second grade to the first, he became eligible for parole, but if he fell to the third grade, it would be a year before he could climb up to second again, and incorrigible prisoners had to serve their full sentences.

It was a bright ideal, and it attracted the attention and emulation of other parts of this country as well as of progressive penologists abroad. However, it never was fulfilled altogether, and soon it began to degenerate from the first high aims. One reason seems to have been the upper age limit; men approaching thirty are no longer malleable as adolescent boys might be. One indubitable obstacle was material: Elmira was a disused maximum security prison, built partly on the Auburn plan, "modified and modernized," partly on the outward-facing architectural plan of Cherry Hill, the whole surrounded by a high wall. It was classified as an "intermediate system" and could not begin to have the effect of a modern open prison of the cottage type.

But primarily the reason for the disillusionment and failure of the hopeful American reformatory was the fact that it was founded on custody and security, not on rehabilitation. Within ten years it was just another prison. As John Bartlow Martin puts it, "the American prison is a blend of several earlier systems, all of which are acknowledged failures."

Unfortunately the other states which copied Elmira copied all its defects as well. They too were usually housed in former maximum security prison buildings, they too had high upper age limits, they too were based on keeping prisoners safe. Whether they were established (as most frequently) for the young or were adapted to adult offenders, the same thing happened: neglect, legislative starvation, perfunctory obedience to or complete neglect of the mark system, commercialization of inmate industry—all to the tune of taxpayers' protests that reformatories were "country clubs" or "military academies" or "private schools" better than they could afford for their own sons. The whole indeterminate sentence principle fell into abeyance, parole was unregulated and hence constantly violated. Even the early cottage-type prisons never dared follow the open prison idea all the way; perhaps only Chino, in California, does so yet in this country. Even the advanced Federal reformatories (El Reno, Oklahoma, and Chillicothe, Ohio) today have cell blocks and guard towers manned by armed guards. For the most part, American reformatories have become "conventional prisons for young offenders."

85

In some other countries—as we shall see in more detail in the discussion of contemporary prisons—things went a little better. More often they failed. The Rauhes Haus, near Hamburg, was a hopeful project run by an order of religious brethren on the family (cottage) system. But the Prussian Diet refused it further funds because it was "a religious order in public service." (Another reason was that one of the brethren shot a disobedient boy!) Wittlich, in Prussia, did better; it was the first prison in Germany to employ the progressive stage (mark) system. So did Geneva, and Mattrai, near Tours, in France, which was run by nuns on the family system for boys under sixteen, many of them as young as seven or eight. In these at least we do not hear of the strikes and riots which marked the backsliding of Elmira and its successor institutions here, and which caused one discouraged investigator to say, "the more thorough the investigation, the lower the figure for reform." Reformatories both here and abroad are too often merely preparatory schools for adult criminals; even Borstal is no exception in that regard.

Strange to say, the nearest approach to what Elmira was intended to be is in Soviet Russia. Always remembering that "offenses against the state" are the most serious crimes behind the Iron Curtain, and that adjustment to the ruling system is the primary aim of rehabilitation, the U.S.S.R. has really implemented the original reformatory idea. Its first reformatories, called industrial schools, were established in 1918, largely to house and civilize the "wild boys" who roamed and infested the cities after the war and the revolution. In 1930 these industrial schools were reorganized; the norm now is a school attached to a large factory or mill, with the convicted boys and girls serving a regular apprenticeship. They have four hours' industrial training daily, and four hours' academic classes, besides three hours devoted, characteristically, to attendance in

86

"public activity organizations." The inmates have been sentenced to two or three year terms, and the sexes are separated. There are summer camps and regular leaves of absence for home vacations. The schools are self-governed, with as little official supervision as possible.

Since the western world does not have a monolithic society to facilitate this kind of regimen, we must face the fact that the high aspirations of the early reformatory were far from fulfilled. It was hailed at its beginning as "the birth in the United States of a second penal system." Major Arthur Griffiths, the visiting inspector of English prisons, called it "a regime of extreme mildness," and said that Elmira had "most of the comforts of a first class boarding school, . . . utilized in the process of amendment." Things were never so rosy as that (or were ever intended to be), and overcrowding, legislative restriction on its industry, popular resentment and prejudice, and financial throttling by the state soon brought it down to the bad old level.

But at least conditions were never quite so bad for young offenders as they had been before, and once again America gave to the world a seminal idea in penology.

11

Before we turn to the transition period, culminating in a second wave of reform which led to the gradual improvement of prison conditions all over the world, there is one time-dishonored institution which calls for further consideration, and that is the local (county, municipal, or district) jail for petty offenders and general undesirables. We have caught some glimpses of it already. Now let us look at it in detail, from its origin in the workhouse to its present state. Since local jails everywhere are still, for the most part, about a century behind prisons for felons (today's San Francisco newspaper headline reads: "Feud over Monterey's Dirty Jail"), they belong even now to a discussion of yesterday's prisons rather than of today's.

In a sense, as we have already seen, jails and workhouses grew up together, though jails were first. Both were attempts to do something about misdemeanants, vagrants, and the "undeserving poor." Houses of correction also took over some of the functions of workhouses, and before long all three were thoroughly confused. At first, say Kirchheimer and Rusche, houses of correction took only "able-bodied beggars, vagabonds, idlers, prostitutes, and thieves," then they added men who had been "flogged, branded, and sentenced to long terms" (i.e., felons). Later they admitted insubordinate children, "spendthrift dependents," and finally any poor person who could not or would not earn his own living. Sometimes these latter inmates were farmed out individually to private employers; sometimes the whole inmate body was committed to the exploitation of a single contractor.

This was the general system in Germany, Holland, Switzerland, and elsewhere in Central Europe. Sometimes, in the small German states, the *Arbeitshaus* took in minor offenders from neighboring states, if they were able to do hard work.

Private or state profit, in other words, was the determining factor as to whether a misdemeanant would be sent to a workhouse or punished otherwise, and the avowed philosophy was that having to work hard at unpleasant tasks would be a deterrent from "leading a life of wantonness and idleness." (There is no record that many were so deterred.) They were set to all kinds of manual labor—rasping hardwood for dyers, spinning, making nails, grinding grain, dredging sand, burning lime to make mortar. The original Bridewell itself, in London, from which all other English institutions of the kind took their common name, was of this nature, though the inmates were paid for their labor. By 1579 Bridewell carried on some twenty-five different trades, including the making of gloves, pins, and tennis balls. All this was accompanied by just enough food for sustenance, plenty of whippings to keep the inmates up to the mark, and not infrequently still harsher forms of discipline. Except in Ghent, which has been described earlier, and perhaps in Amsterdam, these workhouses were predominantly not asylums but real prisons and were the precursors, not of the ordinary jail, but of the penitentiary.

It was after the general shake-up in the early nineteenth century that the local jail as we know it today came into being, particularly in England and the United States. Jails as such, as we have seen, date back to Henry II of England, in the twelfth century; he established "places of detention" for accused persons awaiting trial, and to this day city and county jails combine this function with that of a prison for misdemeanants. To put it succinctly, jails have always been places of detention before trial; with the growth of prisons for felons they also took over the incarceration of convicted misdemeanants from the workhouses and houses of correction.

Since local jails are just about as bad now as they ever were (despite some efforts at improvement which will be mentioned later), and since, unfortunately, they are worse in our own country than anywhere else, we need not go far afield in either time or space to describe them. There are 4100 of them, county and municipal, in the United States. (Sometimes, when a city and county are conterminous, county and municipal jails are combined. In the new Hall of Justice in San Francisco, for example, city prisoners are on one floor, county prisoners on another of the same building.) In contrast, all the state and federal prisons and reformatories together number fewer than 150. Only a few are controlled by their respective states. In

89

general they house all persons sentenced to less than a year. City jails in particular have many inmates who stay for only a few days or a week or so—mostly prostitutes, and alcoholics who are thrown in the drunk tank, dried out, and released until the next time they are picked up.

There are notable exceptions, of course, but most of these local jails are unspeakably bad. A third of the inmates are in need of medical care, which they do not get. Another third are there simply because they were not able to pay the alternative fines, just as a smaller percentage of those awaiting trial for bailable felonies are there because they could not raise the bail. Up to 72 per cent have been there once before or oftener—there are county jail prisoners, primarily alcoholics, most of whose adult life has been spent in the local lock-up.

Some jails (Detroit and Milwaukee, for example) take in prisoners from all over the state. Only New York, New Jersey, Indiana, and Alabama have state regulation or control—it was recommended in California in 1916, but never acted upon. In Massachusetts alone, there is a psychiatric examination of every prisoner serving more than thirty days. Nearly a third of these are alcoholics, only 14 per cent of whom are considered "self-correcting." Some states send chronic alcoholics to houses of correction or workhouses instead of local jails—indeed, the workhouses in both Philadelphia and near Pittsburgh are directly called "Inebriate Asylums." In general, the percentage of psychopaths, not psychotic enough to be committed to mental hospitals, is far above its average in the population at large.

New York and New Jersey have county penitentiaries, which take in some misdemeanants and thus relieve the overcrowded jails. Any jail may be declared a workhouse (though few of them are), in which case at least the inmates are not left to rot in idleness and may even receive some elementary learning if they are illiterate.

San Francisco's Public Defender, Edward T. Mancuso, has noted that "there is a greater possibility of miscarriage of justice at the misdemeanor level than with those involving the commission of a felony." In consequence, there are probably more people in jails unjustly than there are in penitentiaries. It has been remarked that juveniles awaiting trial in county jails often have a harder time than do adults. The keepers and guards are inclined to give them rougher treatment and subject them to more indignities, because they resent the thought that minors "have separate courts and will get off easy."

It is not the juvenile courts, or any courts, that can take the blame for increasing crime rates. Says Assemblyman Vernon Kilpatrick of California: "Sloppy jail practices are partly responsible for our increased crime. Our jails are little more than schools of crime. All prisoners in them get a postgraduate course in crime from a variety of experts." Since it is estimated that on any given day there are 80,000 inmates in local jails in this country, their efficacy as schools of crime if not of citizenship and industry can hardly be doubted.

In most jails there is no segregation whatever, except of the sexes (the women's quarters are often so near the men's that communication is easy), and, just as in the old common prisons of the eighteenth century and earlier, first offenders mix freely with hardened criminals. Kangaroo courts abound, and discipline is confined to keeping the prisoners inside the prison. The keepers almost universally are not under civil service, nor were they trained for their work; for the most part they are political hacks who are rewarded for their services by their ill-paid but secure jobs.

To this day, in most places, the fee system obtains in jails, many years after it was abolished in felony prisons. The sheriff or the warden receives a fee or a per diem payment for each inmate. The result, of course, is bribery, corruption, and favoritism. Trusties are not the most responsible prisoners but are those who can make their privileges most worth the keeper's while. A sheriff may draw the money for, say, adequate food, keep the best for himself or retain part of the money, and feed his prisoners on little better than garbage. This is no accusation against any individual sheriff; there are plenty of good, conscientious, and honest ones, but these practices have been investigated and found to prevail many times.

There is usually no professional care for the chronically ill who make up a good part of jail population. Syphilitics and the tuberculous eat from the same plates as the well. "The service of food in city jails often would offend the mores of the most primitive society," says Tolbert McCarroll, of the Oregon Prison Association. "A farmer wouldn't feed his stock that way. If a prisoner is to survive at all, he must forget he is a man. There is no interest in his problems; he is just a bad child to be locked up." That is no longer true of most penitentiaries, but it is the universal situation in the jails, where no attempt is made at rehabilitation.

In most jails filth and vermin, including mice and rats, abound. The prisoners live in corrupting idleness, much as they did on the hulks, with nothing to do but gamble, quarrel, or hunt for some kind of sex outlet.

The jail has been called "the most important of all our institutions of punishment," because so many more persons experience it than ever see the inside of a penitentiary. There are a half-million admissions a year. In 1946 it was found that there were more than 40,000 children in county jails, some of them merely runaways. These local institutions cost taxpayers $50 million a year. The maintenance of each prisoner is calculated at from $500 to $800 yearly —a large part of which goes into the jailer's pocket by stinting food and other profitable economies.

There is terrific overcrowding—one Tennessee jail is a log cabin with just two cots in it, and often up to forty prisoners!—and it is increased because of the fee system. When a sheriff or keeper is paid so much for each prisoner, he naturally grabs all he can—as tramps and hoboes knew very well in their heyday and now vagrants and hitchhikers (and Freedom Riders), who have to keep alert lest they be nabbed and thrown into the nearest local jail.

Men have been murdered in overcrowded jails, most of which have cells only for sleeping, if at all, while other men looked on without raising a hand or crying out. Why not? They are all thrown in together as if into a sewer, and the strongest fight their way to the top. Of fifty-six jails investigated in California, twenty-one were found to be "disciplined" by the kangaroo court system. Women, as has been noted, fare no better than men; in most of the smaller jails they are merely in separate nearby tiers, nearly always with male attendants. In the few cases in which there are matrons, they are entirely untrained, mere political appointees.

Jail conditions in general are not much better in most places today than they were in the Chicago jail when Conan Doyle visited it in 1923. "Sunk in melancholy," Doyle sat down to write a pamphlet of protest, excoriating the jail's absence of light and air ("The architect should be in it.") and its "mediaeval" treatment of prisoners.

If that be possible, the town lockups are worse than the county jails, except in some large cities. At least two prisoners, often more, live in small, filthy cells, in the stench of bodily effluvia and disinfectant. Many have no bathing facilities, but plenty of rats, roaches, bedbugs, and lice.

Some jails have been found which had no toilet facilities except a trough of running water which frequently flooded the floor. And all have execrable food: if none have today the regular diet in Illinois a century ago—two slices of bread, a slice of bologna, and a cup of black coffee three times daily—the beans and stew which are the usual menu are not immeasurably better.

In the largest cities, of course, with their immense jail population, the worst of these conditions do not exist. Food may not be much better, but cleanliness and discipline are. Some of these are almost small towns of their own. Riker's Island, in the East River off New York, by its latest available report admitted about 2500 a year—all convicted male misdemeanants except juveniles, who were sent to Hampton Farms, and "chronic petty offenders" (mostly alcoholics), who went to Hart's Island—and could care for up to 3200 prisoners at a time. Many of the men were indicted for felony but "copped a lower plea." Ninety per cent of them served less than six months. All were under indeterminate sentence, which was fixed by the Municipal Parole Commission. Riker's Island, classed as a city jail, can thus be considered a real prison, with segregation in cell blocks, even though they are decently kept—as few jail cells are.

On the whole, the New Jersey jails are also decently kept, largely because they are not so badly overcrowded, thanks to a law by which all misdemeanants with sentences longer than thirty days are sent either to a state prison or to the Essex County penitentiary. Originally New Jersey's county jails were planned to accommodate short-term felons also, but they never held many of them. Now misdemeanants with sentences between a month and a year can be sent to Essex County, those with a year to any state prison except Trenton, which takes them only if they are sentenced to eighteen months or more. Eleven other states also take misdemeanants into state prisons, leaving for the small jails those with very short terms, those awaiting trial and unable to furnish bail, those awaiting transfer, and material witnesses to felonies. (Alabama, one of these, has for more than forty years had state control of the feeding of all county and city prisoners.) The activating idea seems to have been that penitentiaries were places for rehabilitation of prisoners, jails only for their safe custody. New Jersey, incidentally, has regional jails, combining the facilities of two or three counties, and thus making better conditions possible.

But even when the city or county jail is completely modern in all its material features, it sometimes retains some of the worst features of the nineteenth-century prison. Terrys T. Olender, in *For the Prosecution*, describes the solitary cells in the skyscraper Los Angeles jail: a five-by-five-foot metal cell, in which the prisoner, though "warmly dressed," sleeps on the bare floor, for there are no furnishings except an open toilet without seat or cover, with no light or air except through inch-square densely meshed holes in one corner. There are also padded cells for those whom this punishment does not subdue.

Some of the newly built big city jails have very undesirable features. In the new San Francisco Hall of Justice, for example, prisoners can consult with their lawyers only by telephone across a glass partition, without any possibility of privacy for confidential discussion—a violation of the prisoner's Constitutional rights.

A good many jails now have farms nearby, to which able-bodied prisoners can be transferred. These, if properly kept and well conducted, are an amelioration of jail conditions. They not only provide men with exercise in the open air and useful work instead of degrading idleness (though how much of a farmer a city bum can become in thirty days is yet to be discovered) but also raise wholesome food for the inmates back in the jail itself. Penitentiaries learned this long ago, and the larger county and city jails are beginning to follow their example. Cleveland had a jail farm as long ago as 1905, and Kansas City, Missouri, in 1909; at the latest count there were eight attached to other large cities. North Carolina has farms under control of the State Highway Commission, but so far no county has availed itself of the opportunity to send some of its county jail prisoners there, for an obvious reason—emptying the jails would lessen the keeper's perquisites, and there would be fewer positions to be given as rewards for faithful political service.

The practice of sending out county and city jail prisoners to do public work, or farming them out to private contractors, is almost as old as the jails themselves. Many older persons can remember in their childhood seeing chained men, in stripes, working on the streets or roads. The custom lingered in the agricultural South after it was largely abandoned elsewhere. The end product is the notorious chain gang, which is really a prison road camp, but without the characteristics of the work camps of enlightened penitentiaries.

After the Civil War, with a devastated country to redeem, and with many young men dead or crippled, there was one cheap source of labor—the county prisoners. They were then nearly all white; today most of them are Negroes. They were leased, to all intents and purposes slaves, to private contractors to work on plantations, in building construction, in turpentine camps, and in sawmills. Chained and shackled day and night, they were treated with indescribable brutality. Many were flogged to death, or hung by their thumbs until they died, or left to suffocate in "sweatboxes" like coffins in the summer heat. They were ill and scantily fed, and scurvy was endemic, as were dysentery, pneumonia, and malaria. Men mutilated themselves—broke their legs, slashed their arms, cut their tendons—to escape the horrors of their working conditions. It did them little good in an environment where the sick have been beaten to death for "malingering," and then buried hastily in quicklime without any death certificate. The prisoners slept in chains, sometimes in rough shacks, sometimes in steel "circus wagons." Their guards were the lowest grade of "poor whites," who knew no way of discipline except vicious savagery.

All this is put in the past tense, but much of it still lingers today. Robert F. Burns first aroused public indignation by his revelations in 1932 in *I Am a Fugitive from a Georgia Chain Gang*. His book and the furor it created caused notable improvements in some states, Louisiana and Alabama among them, and North Carolina has abolished leg shackles in eighty-three of its ninety-four penal units. The tendency today is to use prisoners only in labor for public bodies. But there are still chain gangs, and conditions in them in some states are still almost unbelievably bad.

Yet, as Barnes and Teeters relate, three years after Burns's book Governor Eugene Talmadge of Georgia defended the chain gang system because "it kept men out of doors in God's open country where they could enjoy the singing of the birds, the beautiful sunrises and sunsets!"

What of county jails in England today? There are none any more. They have been abolished and short-termers are now sent to local prisons, which are under centralized governmental control. Those awaiting trial are sent to remand homes. England has realized, as America has not yet done, that the county jail is an anachronism. It would be much harder to abolish it here. Lack of centralization, vested interest, tradition, and public apathy stand in the way.

There are plenty of voices urging that the jail as it

exists in America be either ended or transformed. Myrl Alexander, assistant director of the Federal Bureau of Prisons, has called jails "little more than the enforced meeting place for social derelicts who find there the greatest opportunity to infect the casual offender, the unsophisticated, the morally retarded, and the socially inadequate." Louis N. Robinson echoes him: "Of all the abodes for the criminal classes, the jail is the vilest, . . . the most absurd, . . . and the most inefficient."

The Federal Bureau of Prisons now sends most of its misdemeanants to its own eight prisons in seven states —really short-term jails which also take in felons sentenced to not more than a year and a day. All of these are for men only except San Pedro, California. The Bureau believes that "the states should take over all county jails and make them an organic part of the penal system."

Robinson, who calls the jail "outmoded functionally," agrees that if it cannot be abolished it must be thoroughly transformed. There must be places of detention for those awaiting trial—up to 40 per cent of whom are acquitted anyway—but alcoholics, narcotic addicts, prostitutes, and those suffering from venereal disease should be treated in separate institutions. Vagrants, beggars, bums, and "winos" should be sent to farms run by the county or region, where possibly they may be rehabilitated. If that fails, there should be hospitals where they can be treated without physical restraint. It may be that some should never be permitted to leave. As part of a state-wide program, he thinks, farms should be established in all metropolitan areas, and the jails themselves, if they continue to exist, should be placed under centralized control. The fee system should be ended, and with it the trusty system, that "institutional blackmail." If a town or a county is too small or too poor to afford adequate facilities, then several should join together to provide them in the same area.

These institutions should be staffed by trained personnel under civil service, with tenure and a living wage.

Failing any such revolution in local penology, the Federal Bureau of Prisons, which every year sends several thousand short-term or untried prisoners to county jails, has instituted a program of jail inspection and rating. In 1960, it inspected 780 institutions in 48 states, bringing the number of jails authorized for federal use to 829. It also holds annual teaching institutes for sheriffs and jailers, and conducts correspondence courses in jail management. It feels that there has been "a general uplifting of standards," and that "instances of cruelty and abuse of the rights of prisoners are becoming increasingly rare."

Some states have their own programs: the California Department of Corrections does advisory work with county jails. In 1960 it reported that as a result five counties and three cities had established camps or farms, so that forty-three of the state's fifty-eight counties now have one or both, that some counties are introducing group counseling of prisoners, and that three have work furlough programs and others were considering it.

In essence, the American local jail today is just about what the county jail was in England in the sixteenth or seventeenth century—the same fee system, the same filth, overcrowding, semistarvation, promiscuity, the same stubborn insistence by each county on having its own autonomous jail. Despite sporadic and spotty improvements, it is a hangover from the prison system of yesterday, unaffected by either the first great wave of penal reform in the late eighteenth and early nineteenth centuries, or by the second in the late nineteenth and the early twentieth. Perhaps what is needed is a third great wave.

Section 2

TODAY'S PRISONS

1

Reform in all fields seems to come in recurrent waves. First there is a slight groundswell, then it grows, then come the breakers, after which the wave gradually dies away until everything seems to be about as it was before, except that the tidal mark is a little higher.

The first great wave of prison reform came, as we have seen, at the end of the eighteenth century and the beginning of the nineteenth. Then it ebbed, and the penitentiaries which had been thought of as a cure for the squalid prisons of the past became almost as bad as anything in time gone by, and in some respects even worse, while the hopeful reformatory movement for young offenders dwindled into only a variant of the prison system for adults.

In 1870, the First National Prison Congress in Cincinnati drew up its famous progressive "Declaration." The London Prison Congress in 1872 came out flatly for individual treatment of prisoners and announced that "moral regeneration should be the primary aim of prison discipline, and hope always be a more powerful agent than fear." The first stirrings of a new reform wave could be felt. Both of these meetings were precursors of the International Prison and Penitentiary Congress. Under various

101

names these conferences and organizations of penologists were ultimately made a constituent part, first of the League of Nations, and after its demise of the United Nations.

Meanwhile, before the wave reached its apex in the work of Thomas Mott Osborne and others early in the twentieth century, there were appreciable signs of progress in both America and abroad. (Except in local jails, which remained as bad as ever.)

Chiefly these were in the area of reformatories for the young, and women's prisons. Indiana had a separate prison for women in 1873; Massachusetts, in 1879. These and the ones that followed were more in the nature of reformatories than of penitentiaries, though they housed both misdemeanants and felons. Very few states to this day have separate prisons solely for women serving long terms, and even the Federal prison at Alderson, West Virginia, is called a reformatory for women. No state in the Union has a separate *jail* for women prisoners. Indiana's pioneer institution (largely the result of agitation by Quakers in that state) was formerly called a prison—there was also an industrial school for girls, first combined with and then separated from the prison—but is now also a reformatory. (One of the best is the New York City House of Correction for Women, which as long ago as 1930 had separation by classification on each floor, with dining and recreation rooms on each, and separate rooms for each inmate.) However, at that same period an observer from Holland, Eugenia C. Lekkerkerker, condemned the American "clear tendency . . . to concentrate all women offenders into one institution, drawing from the penitentiaries, jails, and workhouses, . . . overthrowing to a large extent classification lines according to offense, age, or recidivism." As a matter of fact, there are many women still in local jails and houses of correction, and some, with sentences of more than six months, in State reformatories. The reason for this anomaly is not that women felons are any less criminal or more educable than men, but that there is an immense discrepancy in the number of male and female prisoners. If there were separate prisons for female felons, most of them would be almost empty. That holds true everywhere in the world; the reasons for it belong in the realm of criminology, not of penology.

Concomitant with the increasingly more enlightened treatment of prisoners was the growth of both probation and parole, both of which were first applied to juvenile offenders. Massachusetts had probation for juveniles as early as 1872, though it was not legalized until 1878 and not made compulsory until 1891. The first probation officer in America was a volunteer, Father Cook of Boston. By a private arrangement the judge would continue the case of a boy who seemed a likely subject for rehabilitation and turn him over to Father Cook to see what he could do with him.

Other improvements were in the growth of the indeterminate sentence (New York had the first law, in 1897) and of the substitution of state use for the private contract system in prison labor. In 1790 Pennsylvania was the first in America to give any pay to prisoners for their work except for houses of correction, in its "public account system." By the end of the nineteenth century some sort of small payment (usually with part of the pay going to the prisoner's family or kept for his release) was common in prisons both in this country and in Europe. (In Germany and Austria, however, it was made clear that any payment to prisoners was to be considered a gratuity, not a right.) Work for state use only is by now the universal system in American prisons; the last lease to a private contractor was terminated in 1936. By 1940, indeed, practically all prison-made products were excluded from interstate commerce.

These last changes, though advanced from the penological standpoint, actually came about not so much as an effort toward reform as through the protests of union labor and industry against competition. The question as penologists saw it was whether work in prison is a punishment (which means the use of "made work," the treadmill, stonebreaking, etc.) or a privilege, an alleviation of the corroding effects of idleness and a method of training the prisoner for his life in society after his release. The latter view won. Then came the thought that if a man does productive work he is entitled to some compensation for it, either in money or in remission of his sentence. This payment was always infinitesimal in comparison with the standard rate in the free world—hence the immediate protests of both labor and industry, and the subsequent establishment of the state-use rule. Unfortunately, there is still not enough work in many prisons for all the able-bodied inmates to be employed. Another consequence is that in many prisons the machines and work methods are obsolete —sometimes even the trades taught are also obsolete or obsolescent—so that they do not provide any real opportunity for men to support themselves after they leave the prison.

One still highly controversial means of treatment of convicted criminals in America has been the laws passed in twenty-seven states providing for the sterilization of sex offenders and in some cases of other habitual criminals. The first such law was passed in Michigan in 1897, but so far as is known it was not acted upon anywhere until the Jeffersonville, Indiana, Reformatory in 1899 sterilized its feeble-minded inmates. Sterilization laws are in general permissive, not compulsory except in Washington and Nevada, and for the most part they have very seldom been put into effect. Between 1934 and 1941, 628 inmates of San Quentin were sterilized (about half of them convicted burglars or robbers), but this was purely voluntary, and a result of the experiments in restoration of youth conducted by the celebrated Dr. Leo L. Stanley.

The second great wave of prison reform, though it operated in all areas of discipline and treatment, was characterized mainly by the growth of the idea of self-government in penal institutions. As with other reforms, it was tried out first with juvenile offenders. As long ago as 1828 the Boston House of Refuge had a system of monitors which was a sort of adumbration of actual self-government, but even that was preceded by the New York House of Refuge in 1824. There a rather odd system was initiated: an inmate who misbehaved could be reported to an inmate "jury"; the foreman of this jury—also a prisoner—judged how many stripes the culprit had earned, after the superintendent, acting as judge, had found him guilty. Then the superintendent himself administered the flogging.

Self-government in prisons, as a matter of fact, grew from the trusty system, which itself is an unmixed evil —but did, in this one instance, lead to a real good. It was first applied to adults in 1885 by Warden Hiram F. Hatch, of the Michigan State Penitentiary in Jackson, who organized what he called a Mutual Aid League which included some determination of discipline by the prisoners themselves. It was not a success and did not last long. The real impetus came from two remarkable men, Thomas Mott Osborne and Lewis E. Lawes.

Osborne was, appropriately, born in Auburn, New York. He became a prominent business man and was twice mayor of the town, but from youth he was keenly interested in penology. He had studied the systems of a century before and observed what they had become in his own time, and though he acknowledged that "what strikes us as obsolete represents what was once a reform of an earlier maladjustment," he was severely critical of both the Pennsylvania and the Auburn systems.

The former, he said, "was to force men to think right;" the latter, "to force them to act right." Of Cherry Hill he exclaimed: "Was there ever a more ghastly instance of religious cant and false reasoning? The theory that the object of the prison discipline is to break a man's spirit is one of those monstrous fallacies which reach the level of blasphemy." He was no less disapproving of the Auburn method, which he compared to teaching a caged squirrel to turn a wheel and then expecting it to hunt out a wheel to turn when it is set free: "the assumption that if right action were enforced a sufficient length of time, a man made to behave properly when not master of his actions will continue to behave properly after he regains his freedom."

For many years Osborne had been a trustee of the George Junior Republic at Freeville, New York, founded by William R. George as a school for delinquent boys. The boys in the Republic were its "citizens," and like the citizens of any other republic they were responsible for the law and order of their "country." It was George himself who first suggested to Osborne that a similar system could be applied to adult prisoners—another instance of the treatment of juvenile delinquents' leading the way.

To find out just what it meant to be a prisoner in Auburn, Osborne, under the name of Tom Brown, had himself committed to prison, stayed there incognito long enough to become thoroughly familiar with conditions, and from this experience worked out a system of self-government far in advance—perhaps too far in advance—of anything that had ever been attempted before. This was quite different from a so-called honor system, which in general, in any prison to date, is just a fancy name for the baleful semirule by favorites made trusties—in other words, a caste system.

By 1914 Osborne had won the interest and consent of the governor of New York and the warden of Auburn, and with their cooperation he founded the famous Mutual Welfare League.

The real discipline of the prisoners became their own responsibility. The prison was actually governed by fifty delegates elected by their fellows from the work and shop gangs. They in turn elected five judges, who handled all disciplinary problems—though an appeal could be made to the warden's court (made up of the warden, the principal keeper, and the prison doctor) against their decisions. Later there were sixty delegates, each serving for three months. They had a permanent full-time secretary, whose office was next to that of the principal keeper. The sergeant at arms of the delegates actually was a chief of police, and he appointed his deputies, all of whom were prisoners. The only areas in which the judges, or judiciary committee, did not function were assault on an officer and an escape. The only punishment they could inflict was suspension or expulsion from the League itself. Since only members of the League enjoyed any privileges, it was a strong deterrent.

Discipline in the shops was in the hands of their delegates; no guard or keeper ever entered them. The League controlled all recreation and entertainment and ran a commissary where purchases were made in token money. An employment bureau was established, and members who were released were expected to help secure jobs for others as they came out, and to keep an eye on them generally to see that they did not fall into criminality again.

The success of the League at Auburn was sensational. On the strength of the enormous publicity it obtained, Osborne was appointed warden of Sing Sing, and immediately established a similar League there.

Overnight the morale of the prisoners shot up. But it was *too* successful: it aroused the enmity of powerful politicians and die-hard reactionaries. The New York Superintendent of Prisons denounced the system as "coddling" of prisoners, and the newspapers took up the cry. Finally Osborne was deliberately framed by his enemies, and ordered to stand trial on ridiculous charges. He did stand trial and was triumphantly vindicated, and he returned to Sing Sing. But attacks and harassment continued, and before long he gave up and resigned. Later he tried again in the naval prison at Portsmouth, New Hampshire, and a modified form of his system of self-government now obtains in the United States Disciplinary Barracks on Governor's Island, New York.

The succeeding wardens of Sing Sing, George W. Kirchwey and Lewis E. Lawes, also continued Osborne's work on a smaller scale and with major modifications. Kirchwey had been a university professor, but Lawes was a professional penologist, who had begun as a guard at Clinton Prison in 1905 and had risen from chief guard at Auburn and, later, superintendent of the New York City Reformatory to the post of warden at Sing Sing. So far as possible, he especially tried to correct the defects which had made Osborne's system an easy prey for the reactionaries.

Osborne was no dreamy "bleeding heart"; he was a practical business man and politician and an informed penologist. But he made one major mistake, and that was to include *every* prisoner in self-government. Hardened professional criminals are seldom amenable to such a regimen. Membership in an organization like the Mutual Welfare League should be open only to those who can be expected to adhere to its principles, and there should at the very least be a period of probation before a man is considered worthy of membership. This fundamental fallacy caused the failure of similar attempts at Cheshire, Connecticut, and Rahway, New Jersey.

An improved version of Osborne's methods proved to

be a lasting success at the Norfolk, Massachusetts, prison, under Howard B. Gill, in 1927. This is a cottage-type prison, and it is infinitely easier to institute self-government in such an institution than it is in a maximum-security penitentiary. The Norfolk system was cooperative instead of completely self-governing. The Inmate Council also included members of the prison staff (though none could be guards or watch officers). Though it decided general policy, it did not discipline individual offenders. However, Norfolk was operated as a genuine "walled community," and even had its own police station and jail! The inmates wore their own civilian clothing and walked as they pleased within the grounds, instead of being marched to and from meals and work. The two agreements on which survival of the system depended were that no contraband was to be introduced from outside, and that there were to be no escapes—and it worked.

Various attempts at some form of prison self-government have been tried out in several countries. They have for the most part failed except with juvenile offenders; there they have sometimes succeeded to a certain extent. But Osborne, and Kirchwey and Lawes after him, brought a wave of fresh air into the stagnant prison system. They inaugurated a second great tide of reform which has not yet entirely spent itself, and which has spread to the entire civilized world.

To see what today's prisons are like and how far they have progressed over yesterday's, let us make a cursory survey of them, good and bad features alike, first in the United States and then abroad.

2

As penology grew into a science, it began to formulate its objectives. "Correctional history has demonstrated," Barnes and Teeters say truly, "that where punishments are severe and prison sentences long, crime increases." It is not a question of "coddling" prisoners, but of studying them, finding out, so far as the resources of modern psychology can do, what in their heredity, environment, and personal history has turned them to crime (whether as an accident or as a career), and how far and in what way these tendencies are remediable. When that is determined, the next question is: since imprisonment for a shorter or longer time is today the current punishment for lawbreaking, how can the prisons be constituted and run so that they will afford those inmates capable of rehabilitation the greatest opportunity to lead law-abiding lives when they are returned to society at the end of their term?

In other words, the object and methods of imprisonment should be, first, the protection and safety of the persons and property of noncriminal people, and secondly, the remedial treatment of the convict himself. "The shift from theories of revenge, retribution, expiation, and deterrence to a theory of reformation of the offender, with its ultimate aim the protection of society," is the hallmark of today's enlightened penology. It is a necessary change-over from the old psychology of free will and deliberate preference of evil, to the modern psychology of man as a complex of influences affecting his conscious and particularly his subconscious mind, and thereby making him and his life what they are.

The trouble is that state penal codes assign the appropriate punishments for specified legal offenses. These vary grotesquely from state to state, so that what is a crime in one is no crime in another, or that a given offense may be punishable by six months in the county jail in one state and ten years in the penitentiary in another. The codes were all drawn up long ago, before the present-day concept of the human personality, and all assume that every man and woman is like every other, with the same motives and the same strengths and weaknesses. They are obsolete, but getting them rewritten is a labor of Hercules. A few states have revised their codes recently with this thought in mind—Wisconsin, for example, in 1959—but for the most part the new code merely cuts out extraneous matter in the old and does not offer the radical change of viewpoint that is imperative. A few other states, Indiana and Illinois among them, are contemplating new codes. However, California's code, despite the state's advanced penology, has never been thoroughly revised since 1870; all that has been done is to add amendments piecemeal, making the code a patchwork which Professor Herbert L. Packer of Stanford calls "the most complex sentencing structure in the country."

All these preliminary remarks are in the realm of criminology, not of penology; but they have to be made because the criminal code of a state directly affects the treatment of the inmates in its prisons. For instance, in 1956 a questionnaire was sent to fifty-eight state prisons asking among other queries what form of punishment was given for bad behavior. Forty-two of these answered that the insurbordinate or the rule-breakers were placed in solitary confinement, with varying restrictions on diet while they were there. There was no exact correlation (nor was any made) between the severity of punishment and the grade of modernity of the state's penal code, but it is significant that it was the more enlightened states that punished by such less drastic measures as assignment to a less desirable job or deprivation of bonus money.

Not one of the fifty-eight answered that they whipped or chained recalcitrant prisoners, or handcuffed them to the cell door, or exercised any of the forms of torture once so prevalent in prisons. However, one need not be a cynic to realize that if such methods of physical abuse did exist, they would be secret and would not be reported. It seems unlikely that the same state which suffocates men in sweat-boxes in the chain gangs never allows a hand to be raised against a prisoner in its penitentiaries. Certainly physical severity is still openly practiced in some of the areas related to imprisonment; for example, prisoners are sometimes brought into court manacled hand and foot, whether they are actually dangerous and unmanageable or not. In one of our most enlightened states, a wounded suspect under police guard in a hospital is strapped to his bed, unable to care for himself at all, and his guard actually has to help the nurse when the bed must be changed!

On the other hand, that there has been immense improvement in all American prisons from their condition even a half century ago is at once apparent to anyone who surveys them. This is most evident, since World War II, in military prisons, which once were bastions of mediaeval discipline, with grotesque machines for punishment like the so-called whirligig, a rapidly revolving cage in which the offender was whirled around until he collapsed. (In Revolutionary days, soldiers, who were all volunteers, might be flogged for so slight an offense as wearing their uniform hats uncocked!) The old-time guardhouse is vanishing, and in its stead the Army, the Navy, and the Air Force (but not yet, so far as can be ascertained, the Marines) have set up retraining programs for prisoners, and the officers in prison service are trained in modern correctional methods at Washington University in St. Louis. But it must be remembered that soldiers and sailors in the guardhouse or the brig are there for breaches of military discipline, not for real crimes; if they commit those, they go to a Federal penitentiary.

Architecturally, American prisons show less improvement than in any other province. Most of the buildings are old and belong to the original Auburn maximum-security category, with cell blocks and high walls manned

112

by armed guards; sometimes the walls are topped by elec-
trified wire, and sometimes floodlights are turned on all
night. The first unwalled prison in the United States, with
groups of buildings instead of massive cell blocks, was the
Lorton, Virginia, Reformatory (which serves the District
of Columbia), in 1915; the first unwalled penitentiary was
the Federal prison at Terre Haute, Indiana, in 1940. As
we shall see, the Federal prison system as a whole is advanced and is a model for all penal institutions. Its Seagoville, Texas, institution is another "community prison" in
the forefront of prison architecture today. Wallkill, New
York, Soledad, California, and Norfolk, Massachusetts, are
other well-planned prisons, though the last is surrounded
by a wall.

Outmoded as so many prisons are, architecturally, many
of them have made what structural improvements they
could. Cells in general are larger and lighter and better
ventilated (though because of overcrowding some prisons
have had to go back to dormitories—a regressive step, since
it eliminates the possibility of any privacy). They are kept
immeasurably cleaner, and most of them have clean bedding changed weekly; toilets and hot and cold running
water in the cells, so that men can keep themselves clean
and shaved; and sparse but adequate furniture so that the
inmates can read or listen to music or pursue a hobby
during lock-up hours. The chief complaint about sanitary
conditions in most contemporary prisons is that too much
disinfectant is used, and not enough soap and water and
elbow grease.

Food in a prison is of the utmost importance. Probably
bad, contaminated, ill-cooked, and scanty food has in-
stigated more riots and mutinies than any other single
cause. Most prisoners are young, robust men; a great many
of them in today's prisons are doing hard manual labor,
and they need three clean, nourishing, appetizing meals a

113

day. We have seen how unspeakably bad the diet was in the old-time prison (beans, stew, and bitter coffee were the staples, frequently ornamented with weevils, worms, insect parts, and rat droppings, and that is still true of most local jails), and we have seen the effect on both the inmates' health and their dispositions. The well-run prison today has an antiseptically clean, well-equipped kitchen, in charge of a professionally trained steward, and the meals are not only nutritious but they are also attractively served and free of depressing monotony. The old-style mess hall, with the men marched in to sit at long tables and gobble slop in record time, is being replaced by real dining halls, with small tables set for four to six, where a man is allowed to choose his company and to take a reasonable time to eat. Some prisons have diet kitchens for diabetics and others with special needs. It is to the interest of the authorities to keep their charges well and out of the hospital and to see that the food is sufficiently good and nourishing (and appetizing, since what is set before one can either arouse or stifle hunger) to enable them to do productive work. (Which is why, in some progressive prisons, the orchestra plays during meals.) Yet even some otherwise advanced prisons do not seem to think of this: in one, the men get their food before entering the mess hall, which is really an iron cage inside the building, and are searched for cutlery as they leave; in another there is a balcony overlooking the dining room in which is stationed a guard armed with tear gas—a very appetizing adjunct to a meal!

The good modern prison does not dress its inmates in humiliating uniforms bearing shameful insignia or their prison numbers. (It is only the experimental open prisons that sometimes allow them to wear their own clothes. In some modern prisons for women, the "girls" wear well-cut cotton dresses of their own choice as to color and are permitted to use cosmetics within reason and to have their

114

hair modishly waved.) Moreover, the uniforms fit, including shoes, and enough is provided to change shirts and underwear weekly. Needless to say, a part of this physical care is the provision of facilities for frequent showers, especially for men who do dirty work.

The last physical attribute of the good prison is its care of the ill. Malingerers are eliminated as ruthlessly as they ever were, but in fact they are rarer phenomena today; it is no longer necessary to wangle a few days in the infirmary to escape the intolerable dirt, disorder, and semistarvation of the rest of the institution. Indeed, there is, in many instances, no longer the old-fashioned sick line, waiting for a quick cursory examination and dismissal with a placative pill. Practically all American prisons today have up-to-date, excellently equipped hospitals and are prepared to handle any sort of medical or surgical requirements. The typical prison doctor is neither a broken-down hack nor a raw novice, but is a man of standing, thoroughly cognizant of the latest developments and able to apply them. Many prison doctors have conducted invaluable pieces of research into medical problems, with prisoners volunteering as guinea pigs. Plastic surgery is practiced widely; sometimes the removal of a disfigurement alters all of a man's future. If the nurses are inmates, they are well trained and competent; sometimes they themselves were once members of the medical profession. In some prison hospitals there are registered civilian nurses or at least a head nurse, and inmates act under their jurisdiction as assistants and orderlies. When it is necessary, specialists are called in for service or consultation. Most prisoners are in crying need of optical and dental attention, and these too are often of the highest quality.

The treatment of the body nowadays inevitably includes the treatment of the mind, for the two are interdependent. Only a few years ago, there were twelve states which had no psychologists, psychiatrists, or social workers in any prison; now nearly all prisons have all three—though there are still far too few of them to meet the demand. Men who were found to be psychotic or became so were once thrown into dungeons, or kept segregated without treatment in sections of the prison like San Quentin's notorious "Crazy Alley," or shipped off to state mental hospitals. They may still have to be consigned to mental institutions, but neurotics and even borderline psychotics can often be helped, if not cured, by psychological treatment within the prison.

After physical and mental care, in any advanced penal institution, comes education, both vocational and academic. We have seen the beginnings of prison schools, in the well-meaning but inadequate efforts of some guard or chaplain or perhaps a fellow convict to instill an elementary knowledge of reading, writing, and figuring in the slow and reluctant minds of the illiterate. All prisons today in this country have some sort of educational department. (As long ago as 1900 the Public Education Association, a private organization, established a school in The Tombs, New York, for younger prisoners—the first of its kind in an American adult institution.) Its nature varies from poor to excellent. Teachers may be professionals, recruited from the local board of education and paid the regular going salary; they may be volunteers (usually in art, music, or creative writing); or they may still, in some instances, be inmates. (Few prisons are so fortunate as Joliet, which for years had the benefit of having an erudite near-genius in charge of its educational facilities, in the person of Nathan Leopold! Unfortunately scholarship is not always a preventive of crime, and most prisons include in their population some highly educated professional people.) Academically, most prisons today make at least an attempt to provide schooling from the first grade to the end of high school, with college courses provided by correspondence with colleges and universities, some of which make special arrangements for students in prison, so that a man could even secure a bachelor's degree—or even study law!—by correspondence alone. Among the subjects covered in most prisons, besides English and mathematics, are history, geography, civics, sometimes foreign languages, and science in its non-laboratory aspects. There are also classes for the handicapped, and in mental hygiene, besides group and individual counseling.

Libraries are a constituent part of education, but here most prisons lag behind. All of them have some sort of library, but too often it is only a collection of tired, stale, outmoded, often mutilated books, distributed almost at random, and leaning heavily toward religious and didactic works. Almost always the librarian is an untrained inmate. The Federal prisons, on the other hand, employ trained civilian librarians in most of their institutions. The American Library Association is trying to bring about a similar standard in state prisons. Most prisons allow inmates to receive approved books directly from the publisher, and to subscribe to magazines and newspapers from an approved list, and many prison libraries themselves stock such periodicals. (In some prisons inmates are not allowed to read local newspapers, presumably because they might gain information about their fellow criminals or about crimes in which they had participated.)

As for vocational training, it varies from a few minutes of instruction on running a machine to well-managed trade courses equivalent to the training of an apprentice in the outside world—sometimes under the inspection or supervision of the appropriate labor unions. It is handicapped too often by the presence in the prison shops of obsolete machines, or of trades and industries in which it would be practically impossible for the inmate to secure work after his release. (That is primarily why San Quentin finally abolished its jute mill, in which all prisoners once had to serve during the first part of their terms—the nearest free agency operating a jute mill was in Holland!)

Not only school classes and on-the-job vocational training and the use of libraries are counted as part of the educational department of modern prisons, but also classes in painting, sculpture, music, various hobby crafts, even athletics, may be educational in their effect. So may the printing, publishing, editing, and writing of prison magazines and newspapers, of which there are hundreds—some of them only mimeographed sheets concerned with local doings, some of them actual tabloid newspapers to which outsiders also may subscribe, some of them real magazines, printed on calendered paper with halftone illustrations and in every way up to professional standards. (The first was the *Elmira Summary*, in 1883—another instance of juvenile institutions leading the way.) In a sense the purely recreational events, whether they be concerts by the orchestra and glee club, theatrical performances, athletic contests (sometimes with outside teams), or movies, telecasts, or radio broadcasts, have an educational value. In at least one case, a large prison conducted its own radio show of talks and music over a district network, with a brief talk by the warden at the beginning and end, for several years, educating the general public as well as the participants themselves.

It must be remembered that all these activities are voluntary; they are privileges which a man must earn and can lose. They are not "coddling," as some of the public accuse them of being; they are carefully calculated means to rehabilitation. It is significant that 75 per cent of prisoners use the libraries, and that they read an average of seventy books a year—nearly twelve times as many as the general public!

From the worst of the old days, some attention was paid

in prisons to the inmates' religious concerns, even before there were regular chaplains and when the only religious instruction came from devout outsiders. It is a well-known fact that nearly all convicted criminals lay claim to some religious affiliation. Perhaps in many cases that is only an attempt to curry favor; but the rarest thing in any prison is a prisoner who is an avowed nonreligionist. The chaplain, therefore, is of the greatest importance in the prison economy. Nearly all modern prisons have resident Roman Catholic and Protestant chaplains; usually the Jewish chaplain is a visiting rabbi, since the proportion of Jews in the average prison is relatively small. Seminaries now train their students specifically for work in a penal institution, and the best prisons appoint men so trained. The prison chaplain has a great deal to do besides conducting regular masses or church services, or accompanying condemned men on their last journey. He often has duties as a counselor, social worker, or even teacher or librarian, besides his availability for advice and help to his "parishioners." Semireligious organizations such as Alcoholics Anonymous have branches in most prisons. There are inmate clubs in which the chaplain is supposed to take an active interest, and he must visit, as part of his pastoral duties, any of his own denomination who are ill or disabled. (The Illinois Reformatory even has a local branch of the YMCA—the only one in any penal institution.)

Other aspects of the progressive prison which are of vital importance as rehabilitative factors are the writing and receiving of letters and the provisions for visiting.

In the old prisons, visiting was free and promiscuous. Prisoners often had their families with them, and their relatives, friends, and uncaught accomplices could visit them at will, as often and as long as they pleased. (Indeed, sometimes if they did not have visitors bearing gifts, the prisoners would have starved to death.) In the Pennsylvania system, of course, there were no visitors at all except the official ones. In the Auburn type of penitentiary, the traditional prison visiting milieu was first organized.

This in all cases established certain days and hours for visits, and a list of the relatives and friends allowed to make them. No others, except lawyers, were allowed access to a prisoner except on special occasions or by special arrangement. In most cases the visiting room was a bare, corridor-like place, with a table running its length, and a wooden barrier in the middle, usually with a heavy screen above it—sometimes a double screen, through which the visitor and the visited had to look and talk. The two sat on chairs opposite each other, flanked by strangers on either side, with no possibility of private talk that could not be overheard by anybody. At the end of the room, on a raised dais, sat a guard who could hear everything said by everybody; he or another guard brought in the prisoners and notified their callers when time was up. Many prisons today still have these screens, and a few have bullet-proof visiting rooms and partitions along both sides of the table equipped with amplifiers. In some cases a man was allowed to shake hands with or kiss his visitor before they took their places; in others, not. The reason for this was to prevent exchange of notes or contraband —it is quite possible to slip a drug capsule from one mouth to another during a kiss. No visitor can give money or any other object to a prisoner; any gifts must be left to be inspected before the prisoner is allowed to have them. In San Quentin, for one, every visitor must submit to a fluoroscope examination before entering, and all metal of any kind must be left to be returned when he leaves; his hand is then marked with a spot visible under black light, to insure that no unauthorized person leaves the prison in the midst of departing visitors.

This rigid system has in some prisons given place to small cubicles, in which a man can have a fairly private visit with his wife and family. In a few open prisons— e.g., Chino, in California—families are allowed to sit together in good weather in the garden and even eat lunch together outdoors, but guards are always present to watch for any breach of the rules. The one disorder they do not prevent, and which makes this otherwise desirable visiting period uncomfortable, is that created by young and frequently undisciplined children; so far no one has thought of having a supervised place in which they can be entertained and kept quiet. The result is a "madhouse type of visitation" which is almost as distracting as the old conversations in public through a double screen.

Most progressive prisons also have occasional tours and visits by qualified invited guests, besides the personnel of theatrical or athletic events brought to the prison by outsiders. These, of course, do not come under the category of person-to-person visiting.

Usually the list of acceptable correspondents is the same as that of acceptable visitors. Rules as to the number of letters a man may write or receive vary widely, ranging from no restriction at all to only one letter to and from an inmate in a month. (In all prisons, letters to and from attorneys or public officials are exempted.) All letters, both outgoing and incoming, are subject to censorship, just as packages are. Experience has shown this to be necessary, but in most prisons the censorship is reasonable, and the prisoner may express himself freely if he does not mind having his personal affairs and feelings read by others. Almost anything is admitted that does not pertain to criminal activities or associations or that would not in any event be prohibited in the mails. Some prisons take special measures to spare prisoners' families the disgrace of having their neighbors (or the postman) see that they are receiving letters from a prison. Recently, for example, San Quentin had its postmark changed so that its official address is now "Tamal" (from nearby Mount Tamalpais). Letters to prisoners must carry their number as part of the address, but many prisons permit envelopes to be addressed to, say, "John Smith, *Box* such-and-such a number." There is usually provision for a man to send out Christmas cards to all his mailing list, even though this may exceed the number of letters he is allowed to write in that week or month. The cards, of course, must be made, or the prisoner must buy them with his own money in the commissary. He must also pay for his own stationery and stamps. In most cases the postage is affixed in the prison office and charged against his account. Needless to say, a man with a history of narcotic addiction has all his mail handled with special care.

Books have very often been written by prisoners—among them *The Travels of Marco Polo, Don Quixote, Pilgrim's Progress,* and *The Ballad of Reading Gaol.* About 1925 there was a pullulation of prison writing, largely due to the encouragement given by H. L. Mencken when he was editor of *The American Mercury.* Today there are classes in creative writing in many prisons, and books, articles, and stories are poured out in consequence. Most of these are unpublishable, but some find a ready acceptance by magazine editors and book publishers. (One recent example was Nathan Leopold's *Life Plus Ninety-Nine Years.*) How to handle this situation is a problem to any warden. Some prisons allow free submission of manuscripts to editors, after the *imprimatur* of the censor, others try to restrict or forbid entirely the submission of a manuscript by a convict serving his term. Some have tried both methods at different times, finding neither satisfactory. (The smuggling out of the manuscript of Caryl Chessman's last book will be remembered.) Nowadays, most progressive prisons allow an author to deal freely with his agent or directly with editors, subject to approval, just as they allow a prison artist to send out his drawings or an inventor to submit his plans and models.

The greatest rehabilitative force in any prison is productive labor. Work—real work, not "made work," which is frustrating and stultifying—is a privilege and should be a right. The tired and the lazy on the outside might think of it as a punishment (which it was originally intended to be), but nothing so wears a prisoner down and lowers his morale as idleness. Prisoners have begged for work, saying that without it they were never tired enough to get a good night's sleep. Nobody, of course, wants to work under bad physical conditions, or at monotonous unskilled tasks.

The difficulty is that there is not enough work to go around. Pressure groups unwittingly did a good job in ending the private contract system in prison labor, but they are doing a disservice in continuing to protest against the use of prison labor for state use. Today twenty-two states make it mandatory for state institutions and bureaus to buy their needed equipment, including printing, from prison workshops, and another, Pennsylvania, allows but does not compel them to do so. This is not enough. It means that large numbers of prisoners have no work to do at all, and still larger ones do not find enough demand for their products to permit reasonable work hours. Many prisoners are employed in maintenance of their own institutions and in raising food for them on the farms; but here again, in an effort to keep as many people busy as possible, the work is spread out so thin that too many individuals have to be set at too few tasks.

123

Despite all attempts to solve this problem—encouragement of hobbies and hobby shops and the like—it remains a major difficulty.

World War II, with its enormous demands for specialized work, showed how valuable, both to the economy at large and to the prisoners themselves, prison labor can be. The slump, when military equipment was no longer needed, was a real setback in one of the chief means of rehabilitation. The more advanced states realize this and set the inmates of their state prisons to such tasks as making automobile tags, stuffing envelopes for Community Chest appeals, or sending out state income tax notices. Each such effort means bucking strong opposition, both from free men who fear (and justly) the withdrawal of their own chance to earn a living, and from the die-hards who shudder at the thought of prisoners' doing actual productive work and long for the good old days when the only prison labor was "making big ones into little ones" as a part of the punishment for their crimes.

Prison work today is primarily a means of rehabilitation, not a variety of gainful employment. What wages prisoners receive (and in some instances their only compensation is time off or the enjoyment of special privileges) is infinitesimal. Sending part of their pay for support of their families is at best only an empty token. In a survey made in 1954 it was found that only Oregon paid as much as $1 a day, and at that not one inmate had a full five-day forty-hour work week through the year. Washington pays the munificent sum of two cents a day! Only 20 per cent of the inmates of Federal prisons do any paid work at all, and all they receive is $25.62 a month.

There is no easy solution, and there is much to be said on all sides. Some foreign countries, and a few local jails here, have found a way out in the system by which a man works in free industry at the going wage but returns to the prison every night and on week-ends. That would be totally unfeasible for hardened professional criminals or perhaps for any felons, though it is highly desirable for misdemeanants. It is one of the questions which must engage the consideration of every forward-looking penologist.

Self-government in American prisons has made no progress since the days of Osborne, and today nowhere even approaches his system except in a few juvenile institutions. Though in some prisons the old vicious, corrupt trusty system still prevails, with its "con bosses" and its ruling cliques, many more have some form of honor system, with elected inmate groups acting in an advisory capacity in some minor matters. In Mississippi and Alabama "honor inmates" are allowed Christmas furloughs at home. But most such concessions are mere travesties.

So far as classification and individualization of prisoners are concerned, there has been immense progress. Most states have diagnostic clinics for convicts beginning their term—some in special reception centers, some within the prisons themselves—where the newcomer is exhaustively examined as to his physical and psychological condition, his educational and employment history, his social standing and attitudes, all of these being studied in relation to his criminal history. He is classified and assigned on the basis of these findings, and is reclassified thereafter at regular intervals, to discover evidences of rehabilitation or the reverse. Classification merely on the basis of length of term would be entirely useless, since sentences vary so widely for the same offense.

The extent of potential reform, which so largely depends on the success of classification, also helps in decision as to the date of parole. Every state in the Union now has some kind of parole law—Mississippi was the last to have a law, in 1944. All but nine states and the Federal government have indeterminate sentence laws. Both of these systems may be regarded as a form of insurance for society. As Assemblyman John O'Connell of California, chairman of the committee on criminal procedure, has said, "The prisoner suffers from a lack of certainty" as to his future, but the knowledge that he has a minimum sentence, after which he is eligible to apply for parole, is a powerful factor in bolstering good intentions. O'Connell believes the period between minimum and maximum sentences should be shortened, to remove one of the public objections to widespread parole.

A man freed on parole is subject to supervision, but there is one area in which we are only beginning to take the first tentative steps, and that is the need for some sort of attention to a discharged prisoner in the first hard months of his return to the free world. Barnes and Teeters say rightly that "every person sent to prison should be released some time prior to the expiration of the maximum sentence." That would mean release on parole for *every* convict and would require a big increase in the number of parole officers, in addition to salary improvements to insure competent ones. The embattled taxpayer can be relied on to fight this enlightened system, but it is already beginning to make a little headway in some few places.

As it is, the path of the discharged prisoner who really wants to go straight is beset with monstrous thorns. If he tells the truth to a prospective employer, he nearly always loses the job. If he does not, he is at the mercy of any malicious informer. Most or all of his friends and associates from the past are likely to be members of the underworld or its fringe, who will find easy prey for a return to criminal activity in a disheartened man unable to earn a livelihood in respectable work.

In most states he has lost his civil rights, unless he receives a gubernatorial pardon, and in Alabama and Nevada even that does not serve unless it is specifically mentioned. Only Pennsylvania holds that completion of a sentence restores a man to full citizenship. With the exception of five states an ex-convict cannot vote; nowhere can he make a contract, take a Federal civil service examination, or hold office in a labor union. In most states he can neither run for nor hold a public office, and in some his conviction is grounds for divorce. Often he cannot get a professional or business license and sometimes not even a driving or hunting license. In North Carolina his petition for a governor's pardon must be posted on the county courthouse door—a free notice of his status to anybody who may not have been aware of it!

Certainly a man who has paid his debt to society and wants to become a law-abiding citizen deserves some attention and consideration until he is able to solve his own difficulties. The odd thing is that it is not the *criminal* we are afraid of, but the *convict*. In 1956 in this country, the latest date for which statistics have been made public, 558,571 felonies were reported in the United States. How many inmates were there in penitentiaries? Fewer than 200,000. By and large, the lawbreaker who is caught, condemned, and imprisoned is poor, friendless, or stupid, or all three. We place almost insurmountable obstacles in the way of a man with a prison record, while our next door neighbor, or our fellow employee, may for all we know have committed far worse offenses and was merely lucky enough to have escaped discovery and punishment.

No survey of today's prisons would be complete without a word about prisoners' participation in patriotic and charitable services. Every good cause knows it can put over a successful drive in the state prison, small as the financial resources of most inmates are. Inmates in a number of prisons have "adopted" a refugee or impoverished child. Blood bank representatives call regularly in many prisons and find long lists of free donors. Prisoners have volunteered for numerous painful and dangerous medical research experiments—and though it is true that they are often rewarded by time off or increased privileges, not so many of us would take a chance at leukemia, malaria, or radiation burns under any circumstances! Prisoners in camps have rendered enormous and magnificent service in forest fires, floods, and hurricanes, and some of them have been killed. The Federal prisoners in Seagoville, Texas, give $10 a month to help the prevention of juvenile delinquency. At Christmas in 1961, the inmates of the Missouri State Penitentiary gave a party for thirty-five underprivileged children, only two of whom were the children of prisoners there, and paid for $2000 worth of toys for them. One prisoner was observed while giving his jacket to a child shivering with cold: "It was great," said another. "Each of us sort of adopted a child." (It is not American prisoners alone who show such social responsibility; the prisoners in Cardiff, Wales, built a center for social study of slum children.)

No progressive prison system can exist without equal improvement in the supervisory personnel. The good prison today has in-service training for custodial officers, on state time, and sends them to institutes for training toward promotion. It pays its civilian employees a living wage, gives them tenure, and sees to it that they have decent working hours and the usual fringe benefits, including medical care and pensions. Many prisons have all of their staff except the warden under civil service. The Federal prison system has civil service for wardens as well, but most penologists think this unwise, since often a better man can be secured if there are no state residence rules. Still, some of this country's finest prison wardens have been men, like Lewis E. Lawes and Clinton T. Duffy, who rose from the ranks in their own states.

True, penal progress is often slow, discouragingly so. It is only recently, for example, that North Carolina established a State Prison Department at all—previously the prisons had been under the Highway Bureau! As Margery Young, a British commentator, has remarked, we have special difficulties that smaller and more homogeneous nations do not have to contend with. "Everywhere [in the United States]," she says, "four sets of authorities are responsible for different kinds of places for the housing of prisoners; everywhere two sets of laws [state and federal, but there are also county and municipal laws] are working, each with its own courts, police, probation officers, etc., and, to a certain extent, prisoners."

This being so, it is no wonder that there are still atavistic practices in many American maximum security prisons. There are dark cells and dungeons and "Siberias" still. There are untrained, ignorant, and brutal guards. Flogging is still on the statute books of some states, though only Delaware retains it as a legal punishment: a few years ago the warden of a western prison was removed because he boasted openly of whipping prisoners. Most prisons are badly overcrowded, and the consequence is fights and murders (San Quentin, now one of the best prisons in the country, as it was once one of the worst, had a rash of them lately), riots, desperate escapes, and what has been called "jail psychosis"—the prisoners would say its victim is "stir crazy"—arising from monotony, the burden of petty rules, enforced idleness, and the general atmosphere of hostility and suspicion acting on minds never too well balanced and emotions never too well controlled.

There is one problem we shall have with us, in this rather Puritanical country, as long as prisons exist. Other more realistic nations have solved it, as we shall see, but we can never be expected to follow their example. If you put enough robust, vigorous persons of the same sex, still in their virile years, in enforced confinement—whether it be in a school, an army camp, or a prison—you are going to have widespread homosexuality. Prisoners are not monks. In prisons, you are going to have what is still worse —the young, the newly arrived, the unsophisticated, as ready prey for older and harder men or women. (This situation obtains in exactly the same way in prisons for female offenders.) In the *relégués'* villages in French Guiana there were transvestite prostitutes. No American prison or prison camp has ever gone as far as this, but the jealousy, bad blood, and violence arising from homosexual affairs are commonplace in prison life.

So there is still much to discourage the reformer and perhaps drive him to despair. The whole concept of the prison itself may be an irremediable evil—"the crime of imprisonment," as Bernard Shaw called it. That we shall discuss later. But while we still have prisons, and with all their obvious defects and errors, no fair-minded student of penology can deny that the American felony prison today (not the local jail) is infinitely better than it was a century ago.

What of today's prisons in other parts of the world?

3

By 1928, there were twenty-four governments represented in the International Prison Commission (later the International Penal and Penitentiary Commission), then affiliated with the League of Nations, and whose last conference under their sponsorship was in 1950. It is now, as the United Nations Congress on the Prevention of Crime and the Treatment of Offenders, a constituent part of the United Nations, and held its first meeting in 1955. At this conference fifty-one members of the United Nations were officially represented. (No government behind the Iron

Curtain was represented except Yugoslavia.) At that time most of the new Asian and African nations either were not yet in existence or had not yet been admitted to the United Nations. There were individual participants from eleven other unaffiliated countries, including Greece, Haiti, the Federation of Malayan States, and South Africa.

A large part of any survey of contemporary penology in foreign countries must be derived from the proceedings of this Congress and from other regional conferences in specific areas. In general, one may say that the basic principles of today's penology were derived from the very advanced (and then pretty unrealistic) Cincinnati Declaration of Principles, in 1870. The Standard Minimum Rules for the Treatment of Prisoners, laid down by the United Nations at this Congress and subject to approval by the participants' home governments (the European Consultative Group approved them at once) follow the Cincinnati Declaration fairly closely, with modifications arising from further advances in penological thought. They include: classification by age, sex, and probable reformability; individualization in the treatment of prisoners; the encouragement of self-respect and personal responsibility; productive work and training for self-support by work after release; moral, mental, and vocational education; and treatment "outside normal prison buildings" wherever possible. They include also, or take for granted, such things as sanitation, light and air, good food, and the absence of brutal physical punishment.

According to these official reports, let us look briefly at what the prison system is like in some of these countries today—always remembering that claims may be more honored in the breach than in the observance, especially in totalitarian countries and those under the rule of a dictator. One other thing must be remembered: in general, prisons outside the United States are much smaller than those to which we are accustomed, which is no credit to us, but quite the opposite. The terrific overcrowding of our penitentiaries is an indictment in more ways than one.

As might be expected, the present penal system of the United Kingdom and of the British Commonwealth, once as bad as any, is now in the very forefront of penology. This being so, it would be mere repetition to note the points in which England (and Scotland and Wales) carry out the recommendations of advanced penology, and emphasis will be laid mostly on characteristics of the prison system which are unusual or peculiar to this one nation. (The same limitation will obtain when we discuss the prisons of other foreign countries and will also to some extent govern the selection of countries to be mentioned.)

In the first place, prison classification in the United States means treatment of each prisoner as an individual, to be assigned where his chances for rehabilitation seem to be best. But in England the term is employed to describe what may be called "vertical" divisions. These include "star class" prisoners (first offenders) and "ordinary" prisoners, also all prisoners under the age of twenty sentenced for not more than one year.

In addition to the Borstals and other institutions for juveniles, which will be discussed later, there are local prisons, corresponding to our (and their former) jails; regional prisons, corresponding to our reformatories; and central prisons, corresponding to our penitentiaries. In all of these the inmates are "horizontally" divided into maximum, medium, or minimum custody.

All convicted persons go first to the nearest local prison, institutions which have been compared to checkrooms or postoffices, concentration points for future delivery. There are twenty-five of these, eight of them for "star prisoners" and civil cases, and five of the latter are open institutions. There are five regional prisons for men, only two of which

132

are open, but even the closed prisons have camps; two, besides a wing of one of the central prisons, for young men under 23; and two small open regional prisons for women. There is a central prison for female offenders, both "star" and "ordinary," but in practice women amenable to discipline are sent to the open regional prisons. Two of the central prisons are for star prisoners only—Wakefield and Leyhill; Dartmoor is for ordinary prisoners. In all of these the different classes are kept strictly segregated.

England still imprisons for debt, and in 1962 a special open prison, Drake Hall, was established for debtors. The majority of these are people who have failed to keep up payments on the installment (or what the English call the hire purchase) system. This is only a last resort, for recalcitrant persons financially able to pay, but the pernicious effects of too easy credit may be seen from the fact that in 1946 there were only 243 persons in England and Wales sent to prison for debt (which included also maintenance and alimony cases), whereas by 1960 the figure had rocketed to 5675. Scotland does not imprison for debt, but merely orders debtors to pay up—presumably those who fail to do so could be imprisoned for contempt of court.

From 1938 until 1948 England also tried a preventive correction system for habitual criminals, with fourteen years' maximum sentence, but it was proved a failure and abolished.

English treatment of juvenile delinquents is enlightened. No boy or girl under sixteen, nor any misdemeanant (tried in the lower courts) under twenty-one, is ever sent to prison. There are state remand homes for those under seventeen, remand centers for those between seventeen and twenty-three, and for insubordinate youngsters between fourteen and seventeen. There are also compulsory attendance centers for those between twelve and twenty-one, which must be attended in the evenings and on week-ends, for sixty hours, spread over a six-month period. Offenders between sixteen and twenty-one can also be ordered to Howard Houses for six months; these are residential hostels in which they must live, while they work outside, and after the six months there, they live under supervision for six months more.

Considerable discretion is left to the judges in ordering the type of detention for juvenile offenders. They may be sent at the court's judgment to any of these institutions, or to "approved schools" for those under sixteen, or Borstals or farm camps, or given probation for from one to three years. In Borstals or other institutions confinement is for not more than a year, with a review after six months. Offenders are also encouraged to make good "any monetary loss caused by their actions."

As early as 1891 a number of penal improvements were made: prisoners were enabled to earn remission of up to one-sixth of their sentences if the sentence was for more than a month; "made labor" and "excessive corporal punishment" were abolished; and persons sent to prison in default of payment of fines were released on part payment only. There were subsequent Criminal Acts, each of which embodied some reforms, but, as Gordon Rose has said, the exigencies of World War II "put the prison reform clock back almost to 1922." The setbacks were made up for by the forward-looking Criminal Justice Act of 1948, whose primary purpose, says Sir Lionel W. Fox, formerly chairman of the Prison Commission, was "to keep people out of prison," or, if they were imprisoned, to be sent there "*as* a punishment, but not *for* punishment."

This Act ended all progressive stage systems based on deterrence instead of on rehabilitation. Now, out of a preliminary "out of stage" period, all prisoners are "in stage," and remission of sentence or transfer to lesser security institutions depends entirely upon their own conduct. Moreover, many things, such as schools, libraries, visits, and letters, which were formerly looked upon as privileges, are now considered the prisoner's rights.

The ideal is a forty-hour work week for all at productive labor, but English prisons are overcrowded just as ours are (the prison population rose from 10,000–11,000 in 1938 to 23,000–24,000 in 1954), and sometimes twenty-two hours a week is all that can be managed. In the same way, the rule of one man to a cell has had to be abandoned from lack of space, and sometimes the cells have as many as three men in them. (Cells, however, are used only for sleeping, except in Dartmoor, which contains mostly professional and habitual criminals.)

English prisons have most of the amenities of the most progressive American ones—education up to reading for the University of London examinations; classes in art, music, and handicrafts; bands and orchestras, dramatic and choral societies, radio, etc. In some ways they are better; for example, the prison libraries are branches of the local public libraries. The daily papers are on file in the dining rooms (England, unlike the United States, has both local and national newspapers), and prisoners may subscribe to any periodicals. There is no actual self-government, but convict "leaders" keep the common rooms clean and escort prisoners to and from classes. Meals are well served and good table manners are absolutely required. Men must shave daily and may comb their hair as they please; women are allowed hairdressing and cosmetics.

The pay for prison work is small, but it is all paid for. The first open prison, Wakefield, found that when second (higher) class inmates were paid for their work, with one-fifth of their earnings going into a general fund, production went up 80 per cent; in consequence the system was extended to all classes and all prisons.

English prisons until recently still employed corporal

punishment, though it was much milder and more rarely inflicted than in the past. Punishment now may include restriction of diet and exercise or deprivation of a mattress.

The government is concerned over the rise of crime and the consequent overcrowding of all types of penal institutions. It has started an investigation of the alarming number of escapes—not from the prisons themselves but from camps, working parties, hospitals, and in transport. There were 122 of these in 1960, and they threaten the whole system of open prisons and minimum security. It is also building new institutions of every type as fast as possible to cope with the rise in prison population. (Today this has reached a peak of nearly 26,500, a matter for grave concern in so traditionally law-abiding a country.)

For this reason among others, prisoners are not simply released at the end of their terms and left to fend for themselves. The Corrective After Care Association keeps special watch over recidivists. Those considered potentially most capable of rehabilitation are sent for corrective training to an open regional training prison. The less amenable go to a closed regional training prison, and the least so to an ordinary central training prison where, unlike the first two, they are segregated from the ordinary prisoners. The sentence is usually for three years, with four the maximum, and recidivists may earn up to one-third remission, after which they are released on conditional license (equivalent to parole).

The Commission which supervises this system also co-ordinates the work of all Discharged Prisoners' Aid Societies, both local and national. Ever since the days of John Howard and Elizabeth Fry, volunteer work for prisoners, both before and after their release, has played a major part in English penal reform. The Howard Association was founded in 1896, with forty-two members, but at first only a few of these took an active part. The Association was really kept alive by the devoted work of its secretary, William Tallock. Tallock was a Quaker and was also secretary of the Society for the Abolition of Capital Punishment. His advocacy of such measures as "reformatory and economic labor" in prisons influenced many of the subsequent improvements. One of his beliefs, which might be worth trying out somewhere, sometime, met with no response. He thought all sentences for the same offense should be cumulative: e.g., a man convicted of burglary for the first time might receive, say, a year; the second time it would be two years, the third, three, and so on.

The Penal Reform League, founded in 1907, supplemented the work of the Howard Association. Its secretary, Arthur St. John, a follower of Leo Tolstoy, was instrumental in passing the Prevention of Crime Bill in 1908, which instituted the Borstal system for young offenders. In 1921 the two organizations were amalgamated as the Howard League for Penal Reform. The League enjoys a quasi-official recognition (it sent representatives, for instance, to the United Nations Congress on the Prevention of Crime and the Treatment of Offenders) and is influential in all movements for the modernization of prisons in the United Kingdom.

In general, the nations of the British Commonwealth follow the Mother Country in respect to their penal systems. Canada, our nearest neighbor, is of special interest. Because of its being a very big country with a very small population, its prisons were once very bad. Now they are very much improved—at least in spots. Canada has a further problem in that it is a bilingual country, with provinces that have little in common so far as ethnic, political, economic, and religious aspects are concerned.

As we have seen, conditions were deplorable in nineteenth-century Canadian prisons, especially in the more backward provinces. To this day, they are best in Ontario, Saskatchewan, and British Columbia, and worst in Quebec. But the Dominion government is working hard to improve the entire penal system and is gradually succeeding. As General W. St. Pierre Hughes, of the Penitentiary Branch of the Department of Justice, remarked as long ago as 1919, "No prison should be made a place of horror, nor should the unfortunates who are sent there be abused or ill treated." He recommended abolishment of the stone pile, state-use work with wages when the work was done well, education, including the teaching of "advanced methods of agriculture," good medical care and better food (though he thought inmates should buy their own tobacco if they wanted to smoke), and the establishment of prison libraries. The fact that all these things were lacking at a time when most English and United States prisons had them is a sufficient commentary. He also advocated separate prisons for the criminally insane and a prison for women in Ontario. Hughes wanted guards to have at least three months' training, with further special training as a prerequisite for promotion.

Most of these recommendations were eventually carried out, though no wages were paid until 1930. Probation had its beginning in Canada in 1928, with the start of a strong centralized penal administration.

The first modern prison in Canada was Prince Albert, in Saskatchewan, projected from 1911 but not opened until 1922. Since 1930, a number of new institutions have been built, with others planned for the future. There are now three open minimum security camps. Women are still housed in provincial prisons, but under federal care. (The Elizabeth Fry Society of Kingston, Ontario, has been a leading influence in their welfare in that prison.) There are reformatories, on the cottage system, and industrial schools and farms for juveniles. (Alberta sends boys who escape from industrial schools to the local jails.) There is now education for all illiterates and those below the maximum age for compulsory schooling. There is also a system of vocational education to a standard "acceptable to labor authorities," and of social "re-education," carried on largely through group counseling.

There has been great improvement in staff training and working conditions. Guards at one time had no holidays at all and were so poorly paid that few competent persons cared to enter the service. Now there is a Staff College, besides local in-service centers for staff training—which in Quebec is given in French.

But perhaps the most marked improvement is in methods of discipline. In 1930, C. W. Topping, in his prison survey, found prison officials employing "practically any punishment short of killing an inmate to break him if he shows fight." (He also found violent maniacs and men eighty years old among the prison inmates.) Hosing had been abolished, and men could be flogged only with the consent of the Minister of Justice; but they were still shackled to cell gates or thrown into solitary without a bed and with only bread and water. Now, though corporal punishment is still on the books, the usual penalty for misbehavior is cancellation of any remission of sentence.

The Archambault Report, made by a Royal Commission in 1938, recommended complete centralization under a Penitentiaries Commission, but this recommendation was never implemented in full; there was too much pressure from the public and from the Provincial governments. Those with sentences of more than two years (78 per cent of whom are recidivists) are sent to one of the Dominion penitentiaries, those under two years to Provincial jails.

There are, on the whole, good prison officers and administrators in Canada now; there has been classification of prisoners since 1933. An enlightened top administration is working hard to introduce, against public opposition in the less advanced Provinces, the rehabilitative factors recommended by contemporary penologists, but still, as Topping pointed out more than thirty years ago, the primary object is not so much rehabilitation of the prisoner as the maintenance of "clean, safe buildings." Considering the obstacles in its path, Canada has come a long way, but it still has a longer way to go.

An instance of the unforeseen problems that arise where penology has to deal with primitive elements in the population is given in Peter Freuchen's *Book of the Eskimos*. It seems that one Nuralek killed a white trader. He was arrested by the Northwest Mounted Police and given ten years in prison in Ottawa. Nuralek's father "was as proud as a Spanish noble because his son had reaped such reward for his heroic deed from the white men; they kept him in a big house at one of their huge settlements and supplied him with food and clothes without any effort or payment in return." Unfortunately poor Nuralek contracted tuberculosis and died soon after his release.

In New Zealand there are far fewer problems than those facing Canada, and the consequence is a thoroughly modern penal system, closely modeled on that of England. The official attitude is that it is "to the interest of the community, as well as that of the offender, to demand that . . . the time spent in prison be used to bring about the greatest likelihood that the prisoner will lead a law-abiding and socially purposeful life on his release," and his treatment during imprisonment is oriented toward that end.

The Criminal Justice Act of 1955 completely revised the penal system. Boys from seventeen to twenty-one are sent to one of the ten Borstal institutions for not more than three years. Misdemeanants of sixteen to twenty-five are sent to a detention center for three months. There are three adult prisons, in Auckland, Wellington, and Christchurch, and eleven police jails where nobody is sent for more than eight days. All prisoners serving more than a year are on probation for a year more. There is also preventive detention for habitual criminals, with a minimum sentence of three years—fourteen years for sex offenders —and corrective training for an indefinite period up to three years for young offenders between twenty-one and thirty.

Every prisoner in every institution must work. The mark system obtains, and part of the inmate's earnings are kept until his release. Besides vocational training, there is academic education up to the second form—about halfway through high school. Auckland Prison and the Invercargill Borstal Institution have full-time teachers; the others, part-time.

Actually, New Zealand is a very law-abiding country, and has so few prisoners—only 1695 in 1958 out of a two and a half million population—that classification of inmates cannot be carried out very far. It is of interest to note that Maoris make up nearly 6 per cent of the population, but that their number in prison is considerably less than that, and that most of the Maori convicts are minor offenders against property. There are few long sentences, and though capital punishment exists there are extremely few executions.

One unique feature of New Zealand's penal system is that a visiting justice has more disciplinary power than the prison superintendent has, and that any serious punishment has to be by his order.

And what of Australia, once a penal colony? Needless to say, Australia, despite its huge size, sparse population spottily distributed because of geographical discrepancies,

141

and relatively large influx of immigrants from very different national groups, is today one of the most forward-looking members of the British Commonwealth.

Since federation of the six states, in 1901, there has been a dual state and federal control of all agencies, including prisons, just as there is in the United States. There are seventy-three penal institutions in all, including a maximum security prison in each state. (In the old days there was no prison at all, and transported criminals who committed fresh crimes had to be sent to the pre- and post-Maconochie hell hole of Norfolk Island.) Only Capitol Territory has no penal institution at all except a small lockup in Canberra.

Though in general Australia's penal system has most of the characteristics of modern prison systems everywhere in the civilized world, there is strong public resistance against "leniency" and "coddling," and there have been backward as well as forward steps: in 1951, for example, Victoria repealed its indeterminate sentence law which gave parole after serving the minimum term. The most advanced state in respect to prison conditions is New South Wales.

Like New Zealand, Australia has had a small percentage of criminals, but unfortunately it is rising fast. In 1958 there were 6603 prisoners, a rise of nearly 2000 from the year before. Most of the offenses are crimes against property.

Again as in New Zealand, the very small percentage of aborigines contributes a still smaller percentage to the statistics of crime. One interesting feature of the Australian police system is the regular employment of native trackers to apprehend fugitives.

Before the British left India in 1950, they had done a great deal to bring the prison system up to date. There was a Borstal institution in Bengal, for example, as early as 1930. There were Revising Boards to review all long-term sentences after two and a half years as a first step toward the indeterminate sentence. Such improvements were introduced as preventive medicine and the extermination of vermin; the establishment of jails for females in every province, with training in sewing and domestic skills; and prison schools, especially in the women's jails, since female prisoners brought their children with them—there were child prisoners also, as young as seven, since in India a child is considered adult at the age of twelve.

The Republic of India has carried on all these reforms and is endeavoring to add to them. There are almost insuperable difficulties—climatic, linguistic, and above all social and religious, with the dietary problems involved. These inevitably slow up progress, yet it does continue, against all the other obstacles in the way of the young republic. British India attempted a system of classification, and the Republic of India is continuing it, just as it has carried out other reforms like the abolition of shackling and of hard labor as an "educative" part of the convict's punishment.

In a country with India's peculiar problems, a neat adjustment to modern penological methods cannot be expected, and every small step forward is a triumph. The British found that out, and the present government must still deal with some of the same idiosyncrasies. For example, Frederic A. Barker tells how interview rooms for visitors were established, but the prisoners would have none of them; they much preferred "squatting by the wire netting with half a dozen relatives talking animatedly on the other side."

In the former Native States, conditions were much more primitive. Up to the end, there was one state in which the prisoners were released daily to beg for their food in the local bazaar. In another, it was considered bad luck to both the state and its ruler if the local jail was ever empty;

therefore a goat was kept handy which was tethered inside whenever there were no human inmates!

Prison reform, like any other movement, has to adapt itself to local conditions. But India, Pakistan, and Ceylon were all participants in the United Nations Congress and signatories of its Declaration of Principles. Ceylon, which was for forty-six years a British Crown Colony, has modeled its penal system on that of England. It also has an approach to self-government in the Prison Orderlies' League, inspired by Osborne's experiments at Auburn and Sing Sing.

4

Statistics as to prisons in the various countries of Continental Europe vary, of course, both with the size of the country and with its crime rate. (The reasons for this varying crime rate belong in a discussion of criminology, not one of penology.) For example, a survey made some years ago by the International Prison Commission found the highest number of prisoners, relative to population (more than 200 per 100,000), in Europe, in Finland, Latvia, and Estonia. Since the two latter countries are now behind the Iron Curtain, it is impossible to ascertain whether their rate remains so high, but that of Finland—one of the most civilized nations in the world—still does. On the other hand, very low rates were shown in France, England, and Scotland, and the lowest of all (only 19 per 100,000) in Ireland.

Another factor is the long delay in trials in some countries. About the same time that this survey was made, it was discovered that almost as many people were awaiting trial as had been sentenced in France, Italy, Yugoslavia, and Turkey, which may help to account for the relatively low prison population in some of these lands.

The Irish Free State has one other distinction besides having Europe's smallest relative prison population; it

144

shares with Belgium and Sweden a system of short furloughs home for inmates of its three prisons who have "earned" them, or who have good records and are near discharge. Despite the Irish reputation for violence, there are so few prisoners that after the Free State was founded twenty-one jails were closed because they were empty.

The Scandinavian countries, as might be expected, have fully advanced penal systems. What one says about Sweden, for instance, applies equally well, with minor changes, to Norway and Denmark. (It is rather surprising, however, to find that Norway has established a very good training school for delinquent male youths between eighteen and twenty-three, with a two-year term followed by release "on trial," but there has never been any provision whatever for delinquent girls. Are Norwegian girls never delinquent or are they sent with older women to ordinary prisons?) Denmark supplements its own open institutions for young offenders by a closed wing of Nyborg State Prison which serves both as a reception center and as a place of confinement for those who "because of special adjustment difficulties are considered unsuited" for placement elsewhere. In Norway even convicted felons between eighteen and twenty-three years of age can be sent to a training school for young offenders, if the court considers they need educational treatment.

The trend in all three Scandinavian countries is epitomized in a statement by the Danish authorities in 1951: "In harmony with a trend that has manifested itself in the practice of the courts, . . . the Ministry of Justice intends henceforth to try to have sentences shortened and their duration determined with due regard to the nature of each individual case."

Denmark is also very sensible with regard to treatment of the Greenland Eskimos. Freuchen remarks that imprisonment is "utterly fruitless and meaningless" in dealing with them. In Greenland "to this day there are no prisons, although the economic expansion of the last years has made it as modern a country as any. By and large, the old Eskimo way of advertising a felon's shame is still pretty effective."

Sweden's first prison reform act came in 1921, followed by another in 1945. The first of these provided for separation from other prisoners during the first three years for long-term felons, but each prisoner had a cell for his work besides a smaller one in which to sleep. Prison farms were established as a link between imprisonment and discharge; in these the prisoners slept three or four to a room. Corporal punishment was retained, but there were strict injunctions against brutality or abuse. This legislation also ended a humiliating part of the pronouncement of sentence whereby it was proclaimed that the convicted man had "lost the confidence of his fellow citizens."

In 1927 a special institution was opened where psychopaths, not considered legally insane, may be sent for indeterminate sentences "if they are a real danger or harm to society." Frequent recidivists are also sent to this prison, with a consequent drop claimed in the number of habitual criminals.

Danish and Norwegian prisons and the Finnish labor camps have space to spare, but Swedish prisons complain that they are crowded, perhaps because their number is insufficient. (They would seem to us to be far from crowded, but Sweden has high standards.) This may be the reason why most misdemeanants are fined instead of being given jail sentences; if they refuse to accept the "day fine" scaled according to ability to pay, jail is the only alternative.

In Sweden, the furloughs home, given to well-behaved or soon to be discharged prisoners, are considered a right rather than a privilege. Where there is no likelihood of

146

abuse, after a certain portion of the sentence has been served, a prisoner may have from forty-eight to seventy-two hours off, plus travel time, to go to the funeral or sickbed of a near-relative, or to make home visits "where there is strong reason"—e.g., a farmer needed at harvest time, the marriage of a child, domestic difficulties calling for family conference.

The Prison Act of 1945 called for treatment of the individual prisoner "with the consideration due him as a human being." (The word "sanctions" is substituted for "punishment.") This does not mean that prisons were to be turned into country clubs; in some ways imprisonment in Sweden and the other Scandinavian countries is rather severe. Leisure time, for example, even after the three years of isolation for long-termers, must be passed "in private" unless the inmate is engaged in a study, handicraft, or sports group. "Reliable" prisoners are permitted to associate with their fellows but only in very small groups—no milling about in the prison yard as is customary in America. (Refusal of association exists only as a punishment in youth or preventive detention prisons.)

A Swedish professor of criminal law has remarked that "until we can be sure what good a prison does, the fewer those committed, and the shorter the time, the better." Ideally, he says, there should be fewer than two hundred in a prison, and sixty would be the desirable figure.

Old prison buildings are being demolished and new ones built. As a result, a higher type of personnel is being attracted to prison work. Sweden still lacks enough prison psychiatrists, psychologists, and social workers, and its probation officers, who also concern themselves with care of discharged prisoners, are unpaid volunteers. But it does have a good psychiatric facility at Roxtuna, which was opened in 1954 for 18- to 20-year-old "incorrigibles," and the Zetterberg plan, announced in 1950 by the then

147

Minister of Justice, calls for psychological and social group therapy.

In the new prisons at least, all inmates work for the same hours (forty-five in a five-day week) as in private industry, under the state use system, and there is enough work for all of them. They are paid about a dollar a day, tax-free. The shops resemble well-equipped factories. Prisoners even make prefabricated houses for other prisons, hospitals, and army posts. The men can dispose of their own earnings as they see fit and are allowed to find work for themselves outside in other trades not included in the prison shops. Some even work for private employers and simply live in the prison before and after work hours. All except those sentenced to hard labor in a closed prison wear their own clothes. After the three months in a closed prison for all felons, they may be transferred at once to an open prison —or sooner, if they are under twenty-five.

These open prisons have unobtrusive walls. At Norrtalje, near Stockholm, the place of the usual armed guards on walls is taken by a closed TV circuit, with a two-way intercommunication between cells and control room, and cameras on the walls. Guards are armed only by their knowledge of judo. Cell windows have concealed steel bars, set loosely so that any attempt to saw through them would only rotate them.

Swedish prisons are well supplied with books, magazines, and newspapers—in fact, it is compulsory to provide inmates with an opportunity to read the daily papers, in contrast to some American prisons where reading of local or even State papers is forbidden. Prisoners are also encouraged to keep in close touch with their relatives. Their letters, outgoing and incoming, are censored, but the warden may waive censorship in cases where he thinks it safe. The men are also encouraged to make their cells homelike with plants and pictures. In every way (and this is true of all Scandinavia) every effort is made to prepare the prisoners for their return to the free world. Sweden's avowed reform plan from 1934 (known as the Schlyter Plan) has been to "depopulate the prisons," making imprisonment the last resort where no other mode of punishment for lawbreaking was possible.

France, as we have seen, has had extremely bad prison conditions throughout its history even though its national holiday, Bastille Day, celebrates the destruction of that dreadful establishment. No one who has read the revelations from Algeria can consider its present penology enlightened—though it is only fair to add that things happen in war, and to political prisoners, that do not happen in times of peace. But it must also be remembered that France did not abolish transportation, with all its dreadful conditions, until 1942, long after every other nation except Portugal had made an end to it. As recently as 1931 Belbenoit described the Central Prison of Beaulieu, where he awaited transportation, as having its inmates sleep barefoot, clad only in trousers and tunic, under a thin blanket on the bare stone floor; and he described also the dark, damp dungeons of its disciplinary department, where men lay in irons, fed on bread and water. Indeed, up to fairly recent years long-term French prisoners worked in irons, with a fifteen-minute rest period every hour. And to this day conviction of felony in France means lifelong loss of all civil rights, with no possibility of pardon.

Nevertheless, France has taken appreciable steps to bring its penal system up to the standards of other advanced nations. Prison administration was put formally under the Ministry of Justice in 1911, though the move was not implemented until 1937, or the new fourteen-point code fully activated until 1945. The keynote of the new code was: "Deprivation of freedom as a punishment has as its eventual aim reformation and social rehabilitation."

149

Separate prisons were established for those serving sentences up to a year and those with longer terms. In institutions where the progressive stage system was not in force, conditional release was provided for "prisoners who appear to have reformed." Those on conditional release work for three months outside the prison, without official supervision. All prison inmates have to work. All are kept in isolation for the first year; after that they associate even at night. Where the rule used to be that the length of imprisonment was determined by the nature of the offense, it is now modified to fit the individual and his progress in rehabilitation. When transportation was abolished, preventive detention took its place, and this may continue for life, though the possibility of conditional release is always open. Short-termers with less than a year's sentence customarily serve their term in solitary confinement, but some experiments are now being made with placing some short-termers in outside work gangs, or even giving them the half-freedom of outside work, with a return to prison at night and on Sundays and holidays.

France now has two open prisons (one, ironically, in Algeria), three specialized observation centers, five treatment institutions for habitual criminals, and, besides five central prisons, there are five reformatories modeled on Crofton's methods in Ireland. There is an institution at Écrouves which gives apprenticeship training in trades for men from twenty-five to thirty-five years of age, selected according to their aptitude. "School prisons" for both boys and girls were opened in 1947, and a controlled freedom hostel in 1950 as an annex to the school prison for boys. In the same year public observation centers for protective education were established for juvenile delinquents. All boys and girls committed to supervised education receive benefits for industrial injuries or occupational disease, just as older prisoners do. Social, medical, and psychological services are now provided in every prison, and there is a special school for training of prison staffs.

In Belgium, there has been a gradual change for the better since 1920. Up to 1924 long-termers had to spend ten years in solitary confinement—though the hood which solitary prisoners had to wear when they were taken out of their cells for any reason was no longer in use. After the ten years, many prisoners preferred to continue in solitary, since the only alternative was work in association but in silence, as in the early days in Auburn. It was estimated that only 10 per cent of prisoners were working outside of isolation. Psychiatric care was instituted in 1924 (with a "social defense institution" for psychotics from 1931), but there was no "social [including anthropological] investigation" to classify prisoners until 1930. There are now observation centers and school prisons for juveniles.

With the relaxation of the solitary system, the rule of silence was also ended recently. Prisoners are now divided into classes, with segregation of all under twenty-one, all first offenders with more than three months' sentence, and all recidivists. Besides the school prisons (one agricultural) there are adult reformatories, an institution for incorrigibles, prisons for hardened criminals, for those considered amenable, and for those undergoing preventive detention. Besides the establishment for psychotics, there are also special institutions now for psychopaths, epileptics, tuberculars, inebriates, and sex offenders. The prisons for tuberculous and mental cases are on the cottage system.

The uniform of Belgian prisoners has been changed to resemble army fatigue dress. Inmates are allowed to subscribe to daily newspapers, technical periodicals, and illustrated magazines. There are radios in the cells, and there are common exercise yards with facilities for football, basketball, and volleyball. Letters are censored only by random sampling. All except refractory prisoners can now meet their visitors around a table with no screen between them. However, there are still defects in Belgian prisons. The cells are small, and there are no toilets (only the old bucket brigade), but there are showers. Prisoners working outside receive accident and unemployment insurance, but those in prison factories do not.

The most unusual and interesting feature of the Belgian prison system is the "documentation center" at Nivelles, which takes the place of separate prison libraries. It is operated by prisoners for the service of all prisons and furnishes information on technical or other specific subjects as requested, adapted to the education and special interests of the prisoners who use it. Nivelles also contains a permanent "penitentiary exhibit," with scale models, documents, etc., for the use of prison staffs and outside students.

Holland, as we have seen, was a pioneer in prison reform. John Howard spoke highly of its early workhouses and reformatories. Now, at Veenhizen, it has a work colony for four progressive classes of vagrants. Regular penal institutions are classified as prisons, houses of detention, labor institutions, and asylums for psychopaths. There are separate institutions for male and female juvenile offenders.

Prison labor is for state use or for that of "activities serving a useful purpose." If the work is done for public bodies other than state organizations or for private persons, it must be paid for with the same wages received by those in private industry. Part of the inmate's earnings are put in his release fund, part kept by the prison management for the inmate's use, and part disposed of by the Crown. There is a 48-hour work week, and the rule is that work shall "as far as possible serve the purpose of maintaining, increasing, or acquiring occupational skills."

During his first two months the prisoner is obliged to

attend religious services "unless in the case of persons of full age there appear to be objections based on their views concerning religion." Discipline is strict, and includes irons and disciplinary cells on a bread and water diet, but no one may be confined in them for more than four weeks, or kept in irons for more than two, and before discipline is imposed the offender is given a chance to state his side of the case. Sentences may be interrupted, for sufficient reasons, for not more than three months, or in special cases prisoners may be given a temporary furlough "under safeguards." Holland has had the progressive classification system since 1925.

The whole prison system in the Netherlands is under the jurisdiction of an Advisory Council for the Prison System, the Care of Psychopaths, and the Rehabilitation System. This consists of not more than forty-two persons, who are appointed by and hold their membership at the pleasure of the Crown.

Prison reform in Germany, which was flourishing under the Weimar Republic, died a sudden death when the Nazis came into power. (They announced that "imprisonment should be a serious hardship"—it was!) The Nazis officially decreed that punishment should be devoted to the two aims of education and prevention of crime. Up to and throughout World War II the treatment of actual criminals was relatively lenient—they often became minor officials in the concentration camps—while that of political and ethnic "offenders," as all the world knows, was a compound of humiliation, brutality, and deliberate elimination.

Even before Hitler, prison reform in Germany was spotty, since it was not under central control but was within the province of the separate states. In Saxony, for example, up to World War I prisoners might be sentenced to "lathe arrest," which meant that they were incarcerated in cubicles so small they could not stand and had to lie on a floor covered with sharp lathes. In Western Germany today steps have been taken to bring the prison system into approximation to the standards of democratic nations; from Eastern Germany no information on present prison conditions is available.

Austria, for all its *gemütlichkeit,* has always been harsh and severe in its prison system. As Sybille Bedford says, it was "singularly brutal in its dealings with common criminals." The use of heavy chains on prisoners was not abolished until the twentieth century was well under way. Like Prussia particularly among the German states, Austria was very late in liberalizing its treatment of prisoners. And, again like Germany, humiliation and degradation were among its chief penal methods. An instance is given of a small child sent for a holiday to Germany who returned with a bad report. On his return to Austria he was made to wear around his neck a placard reading: "I stole from my foster parents who befriended me." Neither Germany nor Austria has displayed any special alleviation of imprisonment for the young. In the Nazi prison system in both countries even juvenile offenders had to stay in solitary confinement for the first three years of their sentence.

Similarly, Italy under Fascism had a very severe penal code, with extra sentences "for public security" tacked on to the regular terms for specific crimes. The treatment of political (anti-Fascist) prisoners was brutal in the extreme, including transportation to vile island prisons. The Fascist Rossi Code did, however, afford some classification of prisoners under judicial control and instituted wages for prison labor, for common criminals. Here again, a reconstructed country is endeavoring to bring its penal system into accord with modern practice. But the Italian prison system, especially in Sicily, is still extremely backward. So is that of Spain.

Switzerland, in so many ways a most progressive nation, still has some strange social anachronisms—it is, for example, the only country in Europe whose women are disfranchised. Though it abolished capital punishment nearly a century ago, its prison system is far from enlightened. The reason is that there is no one system, but a congeries of systems, each canton having its own. In late years some Federal control has been established, and among Federal regulations now enforced on all cantons are the beginnings of a progressive stage system, pay for prison labor, segregation of the sexes in all prisons, and provisions for interruption of imprisonment "for urgent reasons." Flogging is forbidden in all cantons, and some have other modern prison features; the canton of Berne, for example, has a farm-prison at Witzwill. But in some less progressive cantons, dungeons, chains, and straitjackets for recalcitrant prisoners were in use as late as 1937.

Greece, rather surprisingly, has a penal system with some most advanced attributes, especially with regard to young offenders. A boy under nineteen who is held for trial or already serving a sentence may be transferred to a training school, while his sentence or trial is suspended. If he is considered rehabilitated after a term in the school he may be granted release on parole or the charge may be dismissed altogether, and the time he has spent in the school counts on his sentence. Greece also has had prison camps and farms for the past forty years.

When it comes to adult offenders, sentences of not more than a year may be suspended if the convicted man is either under twenty-one or over seventy; and a sentence of any length may be suspended after a third of it has been served —with the exception of those convicted of smuggling, brigandage, or counterfeiting, those who in the past have been sentenced twice for more than a year, and those who have served prison terms previously for theft, false pretense, or forgery.

In Yugoslavia imprisonment is divided into "rigorous" and "ordinary." Rigorous imprisonment may be from six months to twenty years, ordinary from three days to five years. The sexes are separated if they are not in separate prisons. Prisoners are usually placed in segregated groups, the members of which are judged to have similar personal characters, education, and behavior; there are special divisions for alcoholics. There is solitary confinement only when an inmate is considered "dangerous to the safety and re-education of the other prisoners," and even then it cannot be for more than three years or a quarter of the term, whichever is lower, and no physically or mentally ill prisoner can be put in solitary.

There is a protective home for delinquent mothers, to which all pregnant women are transferred three months before they give birth, and in which they stay until the child is a year old. Women whose babies have been born are segregated from the pregnant, and there is a special room for the children. Mothers may nurse their own infants. No heavy work can be given a woman for five weeks before and after parturition. When the child is a year old it is put in the care of the mother's family, or if that is impossible it is sent to a children's home, and the mother is returned to the ordinary prison. "The principal method of reforming a delinquent mother is by work"; work groups are directed by an inmate leader selected by her fellow-inmates with approval of the administration. Members of these work groups are not allowed to converse except on matters related to their task. They may not be employed outside by private persons, as under some circumstances ordinary prisoners, both men and women, may be. There are classes for illiterates, besides other academic and vocational teaching.

Every prisoner in Yugoslavia must work if he is physically able, eight hours a day, six days a week. Pay is allocated according to the nature of the work, one-third is kept until the prisoner's release, one-third is his to spend (he may buy newspapers, magazines, books, or food, but not alcohol), and one-third—together with bonuses for overtime or given to those "who distinguish themselves at work by rationalization, innovation, or invention"—goes to his family or other dependents. Prisoners have accident and health insurance. Those undergoing rigorous imprisonment are ordinarily assigned to manual labor "suited to special skills and aptitudes"; if this labor is new to them, it must be very light, and if a prisoner is found to be incapable of manual labor he is assigned to "whatever kind of work he can do." No prisoner can be employed outside except in state or other cooperative enterprises or in public works, and not then until he has served three months of ordinary imprisonment or six months of rigorous imprisonment.

Juvenile offenders are sent to a reformatory, "to accustom them to labor discipline and a correct attitude toward the State and their social obligations, train them for communal life and strengthen those features of their character which will assist to develop in them an inclination for socially useful work, in order to restrain them from committing further criminal acts." All reformatories have either industrial and crafts workshops, or agricultural camps, or both.

Obviously the Yugoslav prison system is oriented toward the political ideology of the government, but (as we shall see is also the case in Russia) it embodies all the characteristics of advanced penology in non-Communist countries.

The Communist orientation is shown more obviously in Czechoslovakia, where the penal code decrees that "any person who has shown hostility to the People's Democratic Order and who does not show by his work and conduct during imprisonment an improvement such as to justify the hope that he will in the future lead the orderly life of a worker" may, when his sentence has been served, be transferred to a compulsory labor camp for from three months to two years. Decisions as to such transfers are made by the Committee on Conditional Release attached to each district court, at the request of the district prosecutor.

Poland has a variation on this correctional method. Offenders may receive a sentence of "corrective labor" to be served without deprivation of liberty. If they work for social or economic undertakings or for the State, they serve in their own home district; if they work in private enterprises the Presidium of the People's Council may designate another place of employment, but it must be within reach of the man's home; if it is in another town the employer must provide lodging. Twenty per cent of the convicted man's wages are taken by the State. The Presidium may also assign offenders to public work without pay, at the rate of one day for each three to five days of his ordinary paid employment.

Poland's prison system is a strange mixture of mediaevalism and modernism. It is almost the last place in Europe where there are no separate cells, but prisoners live, sleep, and eat in large common rooms. Yet it provides for conditional (supervised) release after half of a sentence has been served, or after ten years in the case of a life sentence. It has remand homes as well as reformatories for minors, though if there should be none in the province or it should be inadequate a boy may be sent provisionally to a segregated part of a prison or house of detention. "Educational measures" may be applied to a minor considered still to have criminal tendencies until he reaches majority, which in Poland is at eighteen. There is academic and vocational training, with work on collective farms for young persons, who are to be inculcated with "the principles of community life in a Socialist society." Strict discipline is applied to both juveniles and adults who are "seriously demoralized, or who have committed offenses highly dangerous to society." And there is a grim shiver at sight of an order that "unless necessitated by special considerations and circumstances" no one is to be sentenced to prison under the age of—seven!

And what of contemporary penology in Soviet Russia itself, the guide and mentor of all the Iron Curtain countries?

How far all the regulations are carried out in practice, we have no means of knowing; visitors from abroad are not usually welcome in Russian prisons unless they find themselves sent there as inmates. But so far as rules and standards are concerned, the U.S.S.R. has one of the most advanced prison systems in the world, for non-political prisoners at any rate.

It has certainly come a long way from the Czarist days when in the prison of St. Peter and St. Paul the floors and walls of the solitary cells were covered with felt, and a wire netting lined with linen and paper was set up five inches from each wall, all to keep prisoners from communicating with one another even by knocking. (And yet the Russian penal code in the nineteenth century was milder than that of France.)

No description of U.S.S.R. penal methods can be made without keeping in mind the inescapable fact that treatment is very different for offenders against the State and the Party from that of ordinary criminals. Where the two are in the same prison, the politicals are despised by the murderers and thieves, and when there is an amnesty they are always the last to be freed.

It is the penal labor camps, the so-called "slave labor," that are always thought of first by Westerners. There is assuredly a class character to all criminal legislation in

Russia, and sentences are given according to the "measure of actual danger." To the Russian, public work and penal camps are known as corrective labor, and there is a definite aim of avoiding the "prison spirit" of the old-time transportation. Every offender, political or non-political, who receives more than a three-month sentence may be sent to a compulsory labor camp, and in the Urals and Siberia all prisons have been abandoned and the camps are substituted for them.

Moreover, as Wright Miller has remarked in *Russians as People,* the Russians say nowadays that the camps are almost empty, and Khrushchev "has said publicly that there are 'almost no political offenders any more.' " There are certainly fewer than there were under the Stalin dictatorship. "But the policy which sent millions of 'offenders' to camps . . . has not yet been openly repudiated or condemned."

For the ordinary criminal sentenced to a penal labor camp, conditions, aside from the deprivation of liberty which is always the worst punishment, are far from onerous. No convict need work, but if he does not he loses most of his privileges. Food, for example, is measured according to the heaviness of the work done. Prisoners in the higher grades get one or two weeks' vacation a year, besides emergency leaves for family illness or death, and farmers get three months' harvest leave which counts on their sentence. Workers are paid from 35 per cent to 59 per cent of the scale for the same occupation outside, with no deduction for maintenance, and no personal service to any of the staff is required of any inmate. The camps have general, vocational, and "political" classes, movies, plays, and concerts.

Since 1934 all penal institutions have been the responsibility of the Commissariat of Home Affairs, and each has also a local Observation Committee from the trade unions.

Besides this, each penal camp has a "patron factory" which provides jobs before or after release.

There are still, of course, actual prisons in the U.S.S.R., such as Sokolniki jail in Moscow, which is a penitentiary for men with sentences of from one to three years, and for long-termers who are unfit for manual labor. There are provincial detention points, some of which conduct regular universities, with classes in science, history, and the arts, and with Observation Committees from the relevant professions. These are for minor offenders, whose release is conditional only on their fitness for a noncriminal life.

In the women's prisons in Moscow (known as the Women's Isolator) and Orenburg the female prisoners are not even so free as they are in Sokolniki. In Czarist days (these are both old prisons) they did no work; now all work, and "shock brigaders" are rewarded by having a better dormitory. There is compulsory education to the seventh grade for those who have not already attained it, and an opportunity for university classes in the evening. The guards—all women—are armed, but there is a "Comrades' Court" for minor breaches of regulations. Children up to four years are allowed to stay with their mothers, and a prisoner who is pregnant on arrival is sent to an outside hospital to have her child.

The Soviets have special concern for young offenders, particularly those under sixteen, and everything is tried before they are sentenced to industrial schools. Once there, boys and girls from sixteen to eighteen are taught trades and have academic schooling as well. In general, a minor is given two-thirds of what the term would be for an adult committing the same crime.

The most unusual penal institutions in Russia are the security camps or labor communes such as Bolshevo, near Moscow. These are for young (16–24) recidivists with long criminal records, but there is no coercion in being sent there; in fact, the first members were volunteers. Newcomers are on probation for their first few months, and the worst punishment they can receive is to be transferred elsewhere.

The labor commune, organized around a labor training institute, is like a small town, with its school and hospital, dormitories for single inmates, boys or girls, and apartments for married couples—inmates may have their wives or husbands with them. Members may eat in a common dining room or at home, as they please. They all work, and as in any other factory there are "shock brigades" and Stakhovinists. A "Comrades' Court" adjudicates disputes or rule-breaking. They have their own wall newspaper, and the usual musical and dramatic groups. If they wish, members may stay on in the commune as free workers after their terms are over, and many of them do. Unlike other prisoners, their food and clothes are not given them free; they are considered loans by the State, which must be repaid out of their earnings. Like those in other camps and prisons, they may have frequent visitors and may receive gifts of food or tobacco from them. Mail is subject to censorship, but in practice it is not censored unless there are grounds for suspicion of the writer.

For nonpoliticals at least, penal institutions of all kinds are up to the most modern standards, and in many ways beyond that of some other countries. No solitary cells are allowed any more in any prison, and if some of the old ones must be used, locking them is prohibited. The penal code forbids "any physical suffering or personal humiliation." It is true that an ex-convict loses his civil rights, but that is considered a matter of social protection, not of personal retribution. Ex-convicts whose crime was connected with their former profession or trade—e.g., a cashier who embezzles, an engraver who counterfeits, a surgeon

162

who commits malpractice—can never again resume their past occupations. But that is the case also in Germany and Italy, and (by action of the professional body concerned) in England and the United States, where a convicted lawyer, for instance, can be disbarred, or a convicted physician be refused a license to practice.

The maximum term of incarceration for nonpolitical offenses in Russia is fifteen years, except for death resulting from robbery or banditry, when it may be (though it seldom is) for life.

5

There are two characteristics of penology in Central and South America and other Latin American countries which are at variance with theory and practice in North America and Europe. One of these is the emphasis on anthropology, arising from the fact that most Latin American criminologists and penologists are neo-Lombrosians—followers of the "physical" or "constitutional" school which considered criminal tendencies inborn and ascertainable by study of the physical characteristics of the subject. There have been North American criminologists of like mind, notably Earnest A. Hooton, but they have had no influence on penology in this country. In Europe also there have been some followers of this theory, and Belgium, for one, has made some approach to it in practice, but in Latin America the prison clinical staffs are full of anthropologists. What happens usually, however, is that they make intensive investigations and issue detailed reports, and the reports never go further than the official files; so there is no actual testing of the validity of this now largely outmoded theory.

The other salient characteristic of Latin American penology (though we have seen approaches to it in Europe and even a semi-approach in some prisons in the southern

United States) is the forthright facing of the sex problem in prisons. Many of these countries to the south of us, as we shall see, have made some attempt to relieve the tension of celibacy and escape the homosexuality so common in most prisons, by provision for conjugal visits. (Elsewhere the problem has been dealt with, where it is dealt with at all, by means of home furloughs.) This too will be discussed in connection with the countries concerned.

For several reasons progress in prison reform has been slow in the countries of Central and South America. Before they gained their independence from Spain (or, in the case of Brazil, from Portugal), they were governed by the Spanish Laws of the Indies, one salient characteristic of which was that there were two kinds of justice and two kinds of prison—one for descendants of the conquerors, the other for descendants of the conquered. Fundamentally, this distinction still largely obtains, though the codes of all the major countries have been revised in the past century, many of them in the past twenty-five years.

With almost a score of independent republics, most of them with a history of recurrent revolution and dictatorship, it is surprising that so much, not so little, has been done. The social conservatism of the ruling class is still manifest in all but the largest and most progressive nations—and even they have had to struggle (some of them are still struggling) with totalitarian dictatorships and all that they imply. When the South American nations first began to feel the winds of penal reform, it was in the early days of the contest between the Pennsylvania and Auburn systems. Most of the national penitentiaries are modeled architecturally on Cherry Hill (except Brazil's, which copied the many-tiered inside cell blocks of Auburn), and they are actually called *Panopticos,* but with the exception of Peru, they found their immediate models in the English and French prisons which themselves copied the American ones.

Throughout the nineteenth century either the solitary system or Auburn's association in silence prevailed, and there is still initial solitary confinement in some South American countries, just as remnants of it still exist in England. However, the progressive stage system began to be adopted after 1880, and terms were usually shorter than is the case in North America. Ten years was usually considered the maximum sentence (except for political offenders), though Colombia has been known to give a sentence of up to a hundred years to a multiple lawbreaker! Life sentences are usually commuted to not more than ten years. Labor for state use (called here the fiscal system) obtains in a few places, but the contract system also survives, though under control of the prison administrators. There is, as might be expected, much brutality in these prisons, but little deliberate cruelty. (It is interesting to note that among the few Latin American prisons where inmates have to wear striped uniforms is the *United States* penitentiary in Gamboa, Canal Zone.)

Most of the prisons have modern factory equipment, but wages are infinitesimal (Brazil and Colombia are exceptions to this), and part of what the convicts do earn is allocated to repayment of the victim in the case of men convicted of crimes against property. Most prisoners are illiterate, and schools for the most part are poor; but there are handicraft classes, and the men make many small objects such as bags and belts which their wives and children can sell in the markets or on the street—as tourists to Buenos Aires or Rio de Janeiro have discovered.

Latin American jails for misdemeanants are, if possible, even worse than those in the United States. Nearly all the prisoners are Indian peasants or urban proletarians. Prisoners of a higher rank, who have money, can rent better quarters and have food sent in from outside, but for the average pauper prisoner no such privileges exist. One may say they have been used to no better, but most of them did have a room of some sort, a bed, a chair, a fire, and some means of an occasional bath—all of which are lacking in the usual Latin American jail. The food is so bad that only parcels from visitors save them from semistarvation; and what food they are given must be eaten in the yard (a series of mud puddles in rainy weather), squatting on the ground, without chairs or tables. Yet some prisoners live under such conditions for periods up to five years before their cases are tried. Often neglected children who have committed no crime are deposited in the local jail—sometimes even in adult felony prisons.

Yet despite all this, progress is being made in accelerating tempo. One may be skeptical of paper pronouncements in lands of one-man or oligarchic rule, but the countries (like Argentina) that have shaken off their dictators are rapidly approaching modern penal methods, and others will follow in their turn. The statistics gathered by the diagnostic clinics may wind up in files and technical journals instead of activating reform measures, but some of them do eventually trickle down to the warden's desk, and some of the wardens today are trained penologists. Prisons may be run on a military system, with the inmates lined up at the signal of a whistle when the warden approaches, and reformatories for women and juveniles may be run like convent schools by members of religious orders, but at least there *is* separation by sex and age and the ultimate aim is rehabilitation.

A Latin American Seminar on the Prevention of Crime and Treatment of Offenders, held under U.N. auspices in Rio de Janeiro in 1953, had representatives from seventeen Central and South American and Caribbean countries and drew up a series of "minimum rules" under the proviso that "the purpose and justification of the punishment depriving the offender of his liberty is to protect society against delinquency," not to wreak vengeance on the individual offender. There must be "firmness but no more restriction than is necessary for safe custody and a well-ordered community life." Handcuffs, chains, and straitjackets are not to be used except during transfer, or on medical grounds. Prisoners must be allowed to communicate, and to be visited by relatives and "reputable friends," though "visits activated by idle curiosity shall be prohibited." (A strange echo of the fashionable who used to visit eighteenth-century English prisons as a show!) Prisoners are to be encouraged to make use of schools, libraries, and recreational facilities. There must be freedom of religion, with "every religion" represented by an accredited minister. One humane provision often lacking in North American and European penal systems is that prisoners being transferred or taken to or from court "shall be exposed to public view as little as possible."

The Seminar gave particular attention to the selection of personnel, and to improvement of their working conditions, on a full-time basis with tenure and adequate pay. "It should be stressed that the advances now occurring in penology imply a new conception of the work of the staff." There should be more physicians, psychiatrists, psychologists, social workers, teachers, and technical instructors. The treatment of prisoners should be such as to "inculcate in them the will to lead law-abiding and self-supporting lives" after their release. All should be obliged to work, and so far as possible offered their choice of occupation, and all, especially the illiterate, should have a chance for education.

Though there are few open prisons in this territory, the Seminar urged their spread, with "an absence of physical precautions against escape"—i.e., walls and armed guards. Since the purpose of such institutions is the development of "self-discipline and inmate responsibility," the criteria for selection of prisoners to be transferred to them should be, not the length of the sentence or the correctional category, but the potentiality of the individual inmate, as determined by psychological and sociological tests.

Turning to special features of penology in specific countries, Mexico, in 1920, adopted a Criminal Code the avowed object of which was to be preventive, not punitive, with the chief concern the criminal's "dangerousness to society." Nevertheless, conditions in most Mexican prisons are still pretty antiquated. Allowing for all probable exaggerations, the firsthand description of a Mexico City penitentiary given by one of the informants in Oscar Lewis's *Children of Sanchez* sounds like a page from the prison Dark Ages—brutality, corruption, kangaroo courts, actual torture by drowning and live wires; military discipline, with army titles for officers and trusties; prisoners who buy permission from the officers to sell liquor and drugs; homosexuals who are housed in separate shacks and used as prostitutes by fellow inmates; and much besides that sounds incredible, such as actual hold-ups within the prison—yet it was all published in Lewis's book and so far as can be ascertained has not been officially denied.

There is a brighter side to the prison situation in Mexico, and that is the conjugal visiting which we shall observe elsewhere in Latin America, but in which Mexico was a pioneer. "Deserving" prisoners can be visited by their wives or mistresses—few of the Mexican poor are legally married—for two or three hours one afternoon a week. The Fabrica de Hombres Nueves, in Mexico City, has a special building, much like a hotel, for overnight visits—this time for wives only. In the Islas Marias Colony, on an island off the West Coast, prisoners may have their whole families live with them; 150 out of 600 prisoners have taken advantage of the opportunity. (The same privilege was granted at Noves Prison, Bello Horizonte, Brazil, but so few took advantage of it that it was abandoned. Perhaps getting away from the family is to some prisoners not an exacerbation, but an amelioration, of prison life!)

As we shall meet constantly in Latin America with these instances of so-called conjugal visiting, this may be a good opportunity to point out that with all its realistic handling of the universal sexual problem in prisons, it has its drawbacks. There is no likelihood that it will ever be adopted in North America—and not just because of our puritanical attitude. Even leaves for conjugal reasons would have hard going in this country: a sheriff in a rural county of California has just resigned because he let a prisoner go home to visit his wife; in consequence she became pregnant and immediately applied for children's aid from public relief! Moreover, who is to say that if a man is given time off to visit his wife, this is where he goes? Reference was made previously to the unofficial conjugal leaves notoriously granted from the prison in Parchman, Mississippi. The governor has now put an end to them since one beneficiary was arrested on suspicion of bank robbery and another was found picking up a burglary cache! These strictures, of course, do not apply to conjugal visiting in the prison itself, but one can scarcely envision a Fabrica de Hombres Nueves in New England or the Middle West.

But in Latin American countries, with their different sexual mores, the system seems to work very well. Perhaps the best is the one established in Argentina in 1947. The National Penitentiary in Buenos Aires has a special building, which every inmate with a good behavior record is entitled to visit periodically and to meet his wife there. Both, however, must volunteer—there is no compulsion on one of a couple who may have no desire to see the other. The rooms are well furnished, with private baths and toilets, and complete privacy is assured. A special staff handles the visits; women officials greet the wives as they arrive and brief them, and men search the husbands for contraband as they leave.

Argentina in general has a rather advanced penal system, since the prisons were reorganized by Dr. Juan José O'Connor, for four years Director General of Prisons and now a judge in the juvenile court. All of the country's prisons except the National Penitentiary are in agricultural regions, with farms attached. The National Penitentiary before O'Connor was the only felony prison in Argentina, so that all the present other prison buildings—including a cottage-type open prison for juveniles—are new and of modern construction. Argentina has the oldest prison diagnostic clinic in the world, founded in 1907. There are also three penal colonies. Throughout South America juvenile delinquents are considered "neglected, not depraved." Because of this their institutions are especially good, with education, athletics, art training (even classes in puppetry in Colonias Hogares), and school papers. Young prisoners who prove insubordinate are transferred to a high security annex, El Retiro.

Argentine prisons are most efficiently run (and this was true even during the Peron regime), with excellent medical care, exhaustive examinations at entrance, an adequate work program, and correspondence courses in technical and academic subjects since 1951. (Not all prisons have regular schools and teachers.) But there is no individualization in the treatment of prisoners, and on the whole the system is too regimented and has too much of a military flavor. This military precision is most evident in the maximum security National Penitentiary, where the inmates wear blue and yellow striped uniforms and are kept rigorously in order. The prison is kept scrupulously clean, though all its walls and some of its windows are painted in a distressing shade of orchid; once murals made by prisoners covered the walls, but they have all been painted over.

Negley D. Teeters, surveying the prison system in Brazil, notes that it is uneven, good in some respects and in some places, bad in others. The reason is that Brazil is the only country in South America whose penal system is entirely decentralized; each state—there are twenty of them —has complete autonomy and only the Federal District, in Rio de Janeiro, draws prisoners from the nation at large. Less than a century ago, the only real prisons in Brazil were military ones, under the Minister of War; the rest were only small provincial jails, with all that this implies. The chief penal institution then was a colony in Fernando de Noronha, an island off Recife. The first modern penitentiary was built in São Paulo in 1928. It has outside cell blocks, thus affording light and air, but they are in four-tier blocks and there is no individual classification or treatment. In the main corridor are framed lithographs depicting vividly the evils of drunkenness, and signs everywhere, indicative of the rigid discipline, command: "Be Quiet!" Nevertheless, São Paulo's is the best prison hospital in all South America.

The district prisons, called houses of correction, are really penitentiaries for offenders of both sexes above the age of twenty-one. The best of these is a model of its kind —for example, all cells have toilets, washbowls, showers (probably a unique phenomenon), radio outlets, and push buttons to call a guard. It has a dining room with small tables where inmates can sit with their friends, and in which four meals are served daily—South American meal hours are different from ours. There is a wall newspaper, and there is even some measure of self-government. Conjugal visits are allowed, and the inmate is given the key to the room assigned to him, to insure privacy. Every new inmate is put to bed in the hospital for his first two weeks. All this is in the remodeled Correctional Colony of Dois Rios, on the island of Ilha Grande.

The Women's Prison is the only one in the world without bars. It is completely controlled by the Church, and is run by nuns on the lines of a convent. Women, it may be noted, are not allowed to receive visits from their husbands as men are from their wives; the *leitmotiv* in all women's penal institutions is "guilt and expiation." There are also reformatories for women (likewise run by nuns) where felons and misdemeanants are unsegregated; in some districts the women are merely in a wing of a house of correction, with male guards and attendants. Occasionally small children are permitted to stay with their mothers, but usually they are farmed out to foster homes.

In the penitentiary of the state of Marias Geraes (Noves), as previously mentioned, families are allowed to live in small houses outside the prison proper, but hardly any families elected to do so and the system is practically abandoned. Oddly, it succeeded in Pernambuco penitentiary, at Itacamatá. This latter island prison has a unique arrangement: special script is issued which takes the place of money, is given as wages, and can be spent at the commissary.

In general, in Brazil, prison wages are very low, so that there is no incentive to earn. Moreover, nearly all the prisoners are farmers, but in prison they are taught trades which they will never have an opportunity to practice on their release. In other respects Brazil has many advanced penal achievements. Solitary confinement still exists as a punishment, but no long-termer can be kept in solitary for more than ninety days. Medical and hospital care are good in many institutions, and in some there are movies, radio, bands, and art training. The first criminal laboratory in Brazil was founded in Rio in 1932. As usual in Latin America, its emphasis is on biological rather than on sociological factors, under the neo-Lombrosian influence, but at least its recommendations have some attention paid to them and are not merely published or filed as in some other countries.

Chile, unfortunately, is one of these countries. Its Institute of Criminology is excellent. The warden is chairman, and the director must have a medical degree. It is also the only such Institute in the world where the women members of the staff have complete equality with their masculine colleagues. It is the best in South America, but its findings and advice are consistently ignored by the higher authorities.

In general, Chile's penal system is antiquated, with the exception of its treatment of juvenile delinquents, which is good. It has certainly improved since the bad old days of the nineteenth century, when solitary prisoners were literally buried alive in two-by-five-foot bare cells, with the expectation that they would die there: it is said that only one man ever survived a year of this treatment. The prisoner was known to be dead when the food placed inside his door was found to be untouched at the next visit!

The National Penitentiary in Santiago, built in 1843 and still in use, is the oldest in South America except Rio's, which was built in 1837. It has some good features: a print shop run on the state-use (fiscal) system and a "self-work" shop, the only officially organized one on the continent, where a man may produce articles for sale. Prisoners who receive wages keep 75 per cent of their pay, with 10 per cent kept for them at release, and 15 per cent sent to their dependents.

173

The Women's Prison in Santiago, run by the nuns of El Buen Pastor, is separated into departments for felons and misdemeanants, but there is no other classification. As is usual in Latin America, the atmosphere is that of a convent.

Chile has abandoned its two former penal colonies, in Tierra del Fuego and on Juan Fernandez Island, but there is a rehabilitation colony on Santa Maria Island, in the Pacific, which does relatively little to rehabilitate. Prisoners sentenced for a term up to sixty days are sent to the *carceles,* or local jails. These are as bad as jails are everywhere, and in some ways worse. Most of them have no beds, and the men sleep on blankets on the stone floor. The Valparaiso jail does have a school, but like all the others it provides no work of any kind. The jail in Santiago, the capital, is perhaps the worst in the country. It has no toilets and the men have to relieve themselves on the floors. The jail is seldom cleaned and never disinfected. It does, however, have a training school for guards. (It must be noted that these conditions and others in South America were true when Teeters saw them sixteen years ago, and some of them may well have improved since.)

Men with sentences of sixty-one days to five years go to *presidios,* which themselves are little better than district jails. There are no cells, only tiers of bunks in alcoves in the walls, and those assigned to bunks on the upper tiers can reach and leave them only by ladders. Those with terms of more than five years are sent to the National Penitentiary, which thus has only long-termers. They may be sentenced to "complet deprivation of liberty" (which may mean solitary) or to limited freedom.

Chile has a very progressive children's prison, called Ciudad del Niño. It has cottages as well as dormitories and is modeled on Father Flanagan's Boys' Town in Nebraska. Many of the inmates, however, are not legal offenders but are neglected children.

Peru also has a good boys' reformatory, controlled by a religious order. Woman prisoners in Santo Tomás Prison in Lima are under the care of members of the Third Order of St. Francis of Assisi instead of cloistered nuns. In practically all Latin American countries woman convicts, and frequently the delinquent young as well, are considered the rightful concern of the Roman Catholic Church.

Peru lags behind most other countries of South America so far as its penal system goes. Few whites were ever imprisoned in the old days, no matter what their crimes, and the overwhelming majority of prisoners still consists of Indians. There was not even an inspector of prisons until 1927, and the diagnostic clinic of the Institute of Criminology, which formerly did some classification of prisoners, has ceased to exist. The Central Prison in Lima has an isolation cell block, whose inmates get two hours' exercise a day, two at a time. Solitary prisoners are forbidden to read, though they may work at handicrafts. The prison has a flower garden in its yard, but prisoners are strictly prohibited from going near it! The best prison in Peru is the penal colony on the island of El Frontón. Inmates have the freedom of the island, they have work, a teacher comes two days a week, and they have radios. It may be noted that there is no heat in any prison in the country, but that is no hardship—in Peru one changes climate vertically, not horizontally, and all the prisons are in the tropical lowlands.

Uruguay is one of the most progressive countries in South America in its penological outlook. Its avowed motto is that "prisons shall serve only for re-education, training for employment, and the rehabilitation of prisoners." Being a relatively poor country, it cannot always implement this belief, but it has abolished capital punishment, gives conditional sentences, and has a training school for correctional officers. One peculiarity of its penal code is that there are higher penalties for crimes committed by

175

three or more persons—perhaps an effort to deter gangsters, perhaps political in motive.

Colombia is another small country which is distinctly forward-looking, penologically speaking. Its *calabazos* (overnight lockups) and *carceles* are just as bad as similar places are elsewhere, but its penitentiaries are good, as penitentiaries go. Every inmate works an eight-hour day; those not in shops keep the prison clean. The guards are armed only with clubs, and there are no guards on the walls. There are no dungeons or punishment cells. Teachers and band leaders come from the outside; the canteen sells local newspapers; there are radio, movies, sports, and drama. In 1951 Colombia established an institution for the detention of juveniles awaiting trial; those under fourteen go to reformatories, those over fourteen to ordinary prisons.

Like Mexico, Argentina, Brazil, and Salvador, Colombia makes provision for the sexual needs of its (male) prisoners. Unlike them, instead of having wives come to the prison, it lets the prisoner do the visiting. He puts on civilian clothes and, accompanied by a guard, goes home if he lives in the same city; if his home is elsewhere he is taken to a certified rooming house where his wife meets him, and they spend two hours in complete privacy. If a prisoner is single, he is allowed to cohabit with a prostitute. (In Brazil, Argentina, and Mexico, wives and mistresses only are admitted; prostitutes are barred.)

One important adjunct to the Colombian prison system is the Antonio Narino National Prisoners' Aid Society. This is a consolidation of all prisoners' aid associations recognized by the government. Its members visit both prison inmates and their families and do everything possible to encourage prisoners to keep in touch with their relatives. It is a quasi-religious society, but it lends a helping hand to the material as well as the spiritual needs of its charges and particularly of their wives and children.

Venezuela, though far from modern in its penal system, does have a good institute for the training of prison officers, which, since it was transferred from the military to the Ministry of Justice, has made progress that has been reflected in the prisons themselves.

Perhaps the two most backward prison systems in South America are those of Ecuador and Bolivia. Ecuador does have a good institute of criminology, which studies all convicted men, but since little attention is paid to its recommendations it is of small help. There is no classification. Convicted prisoners are not segregated from those awaiting trial; woman prisoners are tended by male guards; there are punishment cells—the whole dreary story which has been told of so many prisons in the past and still exists sporadically today. The only penitentiary, the *Panoptico* in Quito, was built in 1874 and is in bad repair, dark and dirty, with no beds and no tables—the men eat standing. There is a swimming pool, but it is used purely as a method of punishment! The only penal agricultural colony in Ecuador is in the tropical eastern jungle, and is hardly a health resort or a model farm. As Teeters says, Ecuador has "no realistic policy or system of restraint."

Bolivia he calls "the most benighted of all, with hardly any system." (In justice to these and other countries Teeters reported on in his *Penology from Panama to Cape Horn,* we should be reminded again that his book was published in 1946, and there may well have been radical improvements since then that have not been publicized; both Ecuador and Bolivia were represented in the U.N. Latin American Seminar.) Let us put it, then, that at least in 1946 the Panoptico at La Paz had men's and women's wings, but boys were not separated from adults. The only toilets were outside in the yard, and there were not even buckets in the cells; a prisoner had to knock on his door until a guard came to take him out. Work was not obligatory, but some work was done for private contractors, with 20 per cent of the pay kept for the prisoner's release. Inmates might also make objects for sale, though they had to buy their own materials and were allowed to sell them only to visitors; in this case, however, they could keep what they got for them. Though there was no organized system of conjugal visiting, wives "as a special concession" (which smells of bribery) sometimes visited their husbands in their cells.

The conditions of duality on the Isthmus of Panama, with the Panamanian government and the United States Canal Zone functioning in close proximity, make it difficult to evaluate the prison system very clearly. (We have seen that it is the United States prison which puts its inmates in striped uniforms!) Panama's prisons were formerly completely under control of the police, until an Institute of Child Welfare, with a psychiatric clinic, was established in 1942. They still control the jails (*carceles*) and the Penal Colony on Coiba Island. This farm colony has earned a bad reputation, which is not surprising, as a good many of the guards are insubordinate or trouble-making police officers who were transferred to this post as a punishment.

The political situation in Haiti, the Dominican Republic, and Cuba, both in the past and at present, renders it almost impossible to obtain any accurate idea of penology in any of these Caribbean countries. They have all claimed progressive reforms which are belied by what is known of actual prison conditions under a dictatorship. Only Cuba participated officially in the U.N. Seminar in 1951. And what is one to say of a claim by the Batista government that it had a Social Service for Prisoners whose object was "to obtain intimate knowledge of the personal characteristics and the possibilities of rehabilitation of offenders through research into . . . the social conditions in which they have lived since birth, the home life in

178

which they grew up during their early years, the standard of education they reached, their attitude towards work in their trade or occupation, and the characteristics of the homes they may have managed to establish"? Perhaps, with the Latin love of show, such a service did exist—perhaps it still does under Castro—at least so far as nonpolitical prisoners are concerned; but it is most unlikely that the results of its studies have led to any notable reform in the treatment and discipline of prisoners. The same may probably be said for the National Prison School, established for the technical training of prison staff members under the Ministry of the Interior in 1951.

This rapid survey of penology in Central and South America can at best be only sketchy, but it does give a general idea of the extent of prison reform in the neighboring countries to the south of us. As for the rest of the world, Africa, in its present disturbed state, is not susceptible to investigation. (South Africa, until recently a part of the British Commonwealth, displays, as would be expected, a profound dichotomy—advanced penology where "Europeans" are concerned, concentration camp conditions for "natives.")

In the Near and Far East, though the largest of Oriental countries is now a closed book to the Westerner, information, sometimes of a surprisingly hopeful nature, can, however, be obtained.

6

The Near East is very close to Europe. Turkey, in fact, is partly within Europe, while Israel may be considered a European enclave in Asia. The latter country was not represented in a U.N. Middle East Seminar of nine Moslem nations held in Cairo in 1953 (including Egypt, the only African nation from which fairly recent information on the status of prison reform is available), but it is a constituent part of the Social Defense section of the United Nations. Israel abolished corporal punishment in prisons in 1950. This specifically covers flogging as well as forms of physical restraint.

Turkey's Society for the Protection of Children includes among its regular activities assistance in the establishment of correctional institutions for young offenders. Lebanon also is concerned with delinquent minors. Its laws provide that every community center must have a section for delinquent children.

Egypt under the Nasser regime has, on paper at least, a thoroughly modern penal code. Ordinary imprisonment is short, and (unless the court has forbidden the option) a convicted man may ask that his penalty shall be paid by work for the state done outside the prison. The prisons themselves being fairly primitive, most offenders do so request.

A pregnant woman sent to prison must receive the same treatment, until her child is born, as would be given a person awaiting trial. If a prisoner suffers from a disease that may endanger his life, sentence is stayed until he recovers. The same applies to prisoners who become insane; time spent in a mental hospital is deducted from their sentence. Children under twelve awaiting trial must be detained in a reformatory or a recognized charitable institution, not in a prison. Every reformatory has attached to it a welfare committee, made up of a juvenile court judge as chairman, a representative of the public prosecutor, and an official of the Ministry of Social Affairs. Conditional release may be granted after three-quarters of the sentence has been served, if the prisoner has been well behaved and has some legitimate means of earning his living.

Egypt has one penal provision which seems to be unique. If a man and wife are both sentenced for not more than a year, even for different offenses, have a dependent child not more than eighteen years old, and have a known domicile in Egypt, either may have his or her sentence deferred until the other is released, thus assuring the child or children of a home.

The Middle East Seminar followed the same lines as those held earlier in other parts of the world, with some modifications because of local customs. Turkey, as the leader in penal reform in this area, advocated open prisons, as "an important step in the development of modern prison systems, and one of the most important applications of the principle relating to individualization of penalties." The upper age limit for juvenile offenders was set at eighteen, but it was recommended that those between eighteen and twenty-one "should receive more favorable treatment than adults."

There is no discrimination because of race or color in the Middle or Far East, but political and religious differences create a sensitive area. Therefore the Seminar took note that there should be no discrimination in treatment of those of opposing religion, national origin, political belief, or social standing. (The recommendation, of course, is hardly likely to be followed in the case of, say, an Israeli prisoner in an Arab country, though Arab prisoners in Israel are treated exactly as are nationals.) Other portions of the Minimum Rules drawn up reflect the special nature of the district covered: for example, each prisoner should have "a separate bed and bedding."

"Prisoners shall be kept regularly informed of the more important items of news." "All cruel, inhuman, or degrading punishments and all degrading and humiliating clothing" are prohibited. "Penalties or measures which cause a person to be withdrawn from the outside world are punitive by the very fact that they prevent him from ordering his life as he pleases by depriving him of his liberty. Imprisonment should not in any way aggravate the physical

181

and moral sufferings inherent in such a situation." Its purpose is "to establish the will to lead law-abiding and self-supporting lives." Debtors and those convicted of civil offenses are treated like those awaiting trial, except that they must work; they "are not to be subjected to any greater restriction or severity than is necessary to insure safe custody and good order."

The following year a Far East Seminar was held in Rangoon, attended by representatives of sixteen Asiatic nations. It too announced that the "purpose and justification of imprisonment is to protect society against crime. Its punishment is primarily the deprivation of liberty, with the inevitable consequence of compulsory confinement and segregation from normal society."

As in the Near East, the Minimum Rules spelled out the special conditions obtaining in the countries, ranging from the Philippines to Ceylon, from Japan to Thailand, represented. To the ban on discrimination was added discrimination because of "property or birth." In requiring a separate bed for each prisoner, the recommendation added: "Bed is understood as in accordance with local or national standard." Food should be served "at the usual intervals." Drinking water must be available at all times—most of these countries are tropical or semitropical.

So far as possible, education in prisons should be "integrated with the educational system of the country." Special attention should be paid to the maintenance of the prisoner's family and to the "improvement of his relation" with it. No female prisoner is to be subjected to any punishment which might injure her unborn or nursing child. (There was no prohibition of corporal punishment altogether.)

Opportunities for religious practices should be furnished, but "if any prisoner should object to the visit of any minister, his attitude shall be fully respected."

The recommendations include the training of supervisory staffs both in schools and, as practice training, in actual service. Except in "special circumstances," personnel in direct contact with prisoners should not be armed.

To have abolished corporal punishment entirely would have met with heated resistance in some of the countries represented. Thailand, for example, which established juvenile courts in 1951, has also provided specifically for "places for detention and whipping" of both children and adolescents, and the ordinance goes into minute detail about them: they must not be connected with a prison, nor may a prison be altered for this purpose; whipping is to be on the back of the thigh with a rounded bamboo stick or a rattan cane not more than one centimeter wide and one meter long; there must be a medical examination before and after the whipping, which can be stopped if the doctor says it can no longer be endured. Thailand in general, in contrast to the permissiveness of most Pacific peoples, apparently believes in severity in dealing with the young. There are solitary cells even in child welfare centers, and "light penalties" for children as well as for adults may include hard labor. A child subject to this discipline is a boy or girl from seven to fourteen; between fourteen and eighteen he or she is considered a juvenile—and, it is added, even being married does not confer the legal status of an adult!

Melvin M. Belli, a San Francisco lawyer surveying Japanese prisons in 1960, reported those he saw as clean, with separate quarters for minors. Reputedly, no Japanese prisoner has ever escaped. In earthquakes and other emergencies, prisoners who cannot be transferred to a safe place are set free for twenty-four hours. Few fail to give themselves up again, as both they and those who helped them are subject to severe penalties if they do so.

Sentences are shorter than in the United States, and the convict is eligible for parole after he has served one-third of his sentence, or after ten years for life-termers. Once in two years all prisons are inspected by judges, public prose-cutors, and administrative officials, at which time a prisoner can ask for investigation of his case. In emergencies, such as death in the family, a prisoner with a good behavior record may be given a temporary release. New inmates are segregated for ten days, then classified.

During the Occupation Japan set up a sort of paradise of prisons for American soldiers convicted of nonmilitary crimes. It was called Yokosuka. Its fortunate inmates had their choice of a double or single cell, with a toilet, and there was central heating. One quaint provision was that a prisoner might have five pictures of his family in his cell, or more if his behavior was good! There were religious services, a school, a library, and radio.

Civilian foreigners did not fare so well. Congressman Frank T. Bow of Ohio reported in 1957 that though their prison was clean, there was no heat, no blankets, and they had to sleep on the floor; the food he called "vile," though that may be only because of the difference in cuisine be-tween Ohio and Japan.

And at its worst, this was a vast improvement over criminal procedure in feudal Japan in the Middle Ages, when the entire family of a convicted criminal might be boiled alive in oil!

Japanese prisoners provide their own clothes and bed-ding, except that indigents are"lent" blue uniforms (pad-ded for the fireless winters). Minors and misdemeanants also wear blue; felons wear red. On the front of each is a cloth tag noting the crime for which the inmate was im-prisoned, the length of his term, and whether he is well behaved or is undergoing punishment. (At least, this was true up to fairly recent years. Convicts released after Hiroshima wore blue arm bands.)

There are four kinds of prisons, depending on the nature and seriousness of the crime committed—the least rigorous of which is not only for those awaiting trial, but also for those awaiting execution! Prison officers are trained not only in the usual curriculum, but also in judo and fencing.

The Philippines have shown continued progress since the archipelago became an independent nation in 1946, but there are still vestiges of the Spanish penal regime. They are evident chiefly in the old prison of Bilibid, to which all recidivists are sent for at least part of their terms. Bilibid is a vast industrial plant, and every prisoner is employed, but they receive no pay until they are certified as skilled workmen. All prisoners under thirty must attend school to the standard of the fourth grade. On the debit side, there are no cells except punishment cells, the inmates living and sleeping together as in the eighteenth-century prisons, and Bilibid has a bad record of chains, fetters, and straitjackets; until recently, the prisoners wore stripes. There is no prison for women in the Philippines, and the treatment of women prisoners in Bilibid and in the provincial prisons falls far short of modern practice.

First offenders and well-conducted inmates of Bilibid who have not been convicted of felony more than twice may be sent to the Iwalig Penal Colony, on the island of Palawan, under the Spanish regime the place of exile. This is a large, thoroughly modern farm, and after serving their terms many discharged convicts settle down on the island as free farmers.

As in Ceylon, in the Philippines there is a Prison Scout Troop for young offenders, in which the Boy Scouts take an interest. But the attempts to reform the penal system of the islands are hampered by the backwardness of the parole and probation systems, which are either lacking altogether or exist only in a rudimentary form.

7

Before we leave today's prisons, let us take an over-all glance at the very best penology has to offer at the present stage of its progress.

As we have seen here and there in the previous narrative, some excellent features may be found in prison systems anywhere in the world. Everywhere, as D. L. Howard says, there has been "a switch in emphasis in prison policy from punishment to individual reform." Sometimes it may be a minor matter—e.g., the change in nomenclature in England by which wardens (our guards) are now called "prison officers"; or a highway sign in California that has been changed from "Soledad State Prison" to "Soledad Correctional Facility" (analogous to the campaign to change the name of leprosy to Hansen's Disease). Sometimes it is of major importance, like the varied but realistic efforts in Central and South America to face and solve the prison sex problem, or the special corrective training in the United Kingdom for recidivists who show potentialities of rehabilitation, which has taken the place of the abandoned preventive detention system for habitual criminals. Another hopeful sign in Great Britain is, strange to say, the great increase in the number of inmates of Borstals —it means that many boys who once would have been relegated to an ordinary prison are being sent now to these progressive reformatories.

Many of these institutions "best of their kind" are located in the United States. New Jersey, which has a special "short-term treatment" for juvenile delinquents of certain types who do not need conventional restraint, established an open institution at Hopewell in 1950 (the former Lindbergh home from which the baby was kidnaped and murdered), which is based on social therapy. Commitment is offered to selected young offenders who enter voluntarily. There is self-government, and each boy chooses an individual project which he must carry through on his own, whether it be making a desk, writing an article, or tending a garden. Individual counseling and specially directed schooling are given each inmate. He works in the truck farm or does janitorial work at a nearby state institution, but there is plenty of athletics and other recreation besides. The success of this system with amenable delinquents is shown by the fact that its rate of recidivism is only 19 per cent, whereas at the neighboring conventional Annandale Reformatory it is 43 per cent.

Another New Jersey experiment which is working out is the Residential Training Center at Highfields, which was originated by Dr. Lloyd McCorkle, a sociologist. Here twenty young men at a time are subjected to a four-month course divided between hard work and daily group discussion, with a counselor, of the problems and difficulties they have in common. That is all there is—no vocational or academic education, no organized recreation, no psychiatric interviews. The results have been startling. These are not specially selected subjects, but run-of-the-mill lawbreakers, young but not minors. It does not always succeed, of course; in fact the rate of recidivism is about the same as that of the New Jersey Reformatory for Men: but Highfields keeps them for four months, and the reformatory keeps them for an average of sixteen months—in other words, the same results are achieved in a quarter of the time.

At Provo, Utah, another sociologist, Dr. LaMar Empey, is conducting another experiment, this time in group therapy without confinement. Twenty juvenile offenders are committed to the Pinehill Treatment Center instead of being sent to a reformatory or placed on probation. They must attend for three hours daily after school, and all day on Saturday and during school holidays. They are put to work on community maintenance and improvement projects and have one hour a day of group discussion. Again, the results are excellent.

One of the most heartening and dramatic improvements in prison systems in America was made in Texas. We have

187

seen glimpses of what conditions were like there in the recent past—Texas was one of the places where men mutilated themselves in prison camps in protest against intolerable conditions. Today some local jails are still very bad, but the prisons and the prison farms—a new one, Ferguson, has just been completed and another is in the making—are rapidly becoming models of their kind.

This is the work of one man, the late O. B. Ellis, one of the really outstanding prison reformers of the type of Thomas M. Osborne and Clinton T. Duffy. When Ellis was appointed to head the Texas prison system in 1948, he had already transformed a prison farm near Memphis, Tennessee, from a rural slum into a well-run institution where both crops and men had a chance to grow. He took over the deplorable Texas system with the same foresightedness and industry. In Texas prisons they are said to date all events as "before or after Mr. Ellis came." His successor, Dr. George J. Beto, is continuing Ellis's reforms.

Like Maconochie and Crofton, he instituted a mark system, which he called the Point Incentive Program. Every prisoner is graded according to his accomplishments, good and bad, in work, behavior, sports, and education. His chances for parole are based on this record; every point counts.

Aside from "Pip," as the convicts call it, Ellis's efforts were largely aimed at bringing to Texas prisons and penal farms what was already commonplace in other parts of the country, but which had been unknown there—things like bathing facilities, good housing for employees to attract a better class of guards, modern farm machinery, a special unit for incorrigibles, newspapers and magazines, radio and television. Above all he stepped up the educational program. It is estimated that 34 per cent of the prisoners in Texas have never reached the third grade in school. In 1959, sixty received their high school diplomas. Enforced idleness, the tank, the bullwhip, inedible food—all were ended. (Texas prisoners are still segregated by race in their sleeping quarters, but now they work, study, eat, and play together.) The prison labor income in Texas has been multiplied by eight since Ellis took over. But he was prouder of another statistic: in 1946 there were 126 escapes; in 1958 there were three unsuccessful attempts.

8

Today, despite the marked improvements noted in these other states, California can confidently be said to have the best over-all state prison system in this country. It is a far cry from the conditions that obtained just a century ago, when a San Francisco newspaper commented casually on "the chain gang pumping water from a cistern," while one recalcitrant prisoner who refused to work was "manacled to a gas lamp and compelled to listen to the gibes and taunts of the horde which congregates there." In other words, California started at the very bottom of the prison reform ladder and is now as near the top as is any like penal system—which certainly does not mean that it is as good as such a system conceivably could be.

The ideal, as voiced by Richard McGee, State Administrator of Corrections, is founded on "three basic themes: 1. Crime is a consequence of emotional immaturity, and there are different levels of this which must be treated differently; 2. There should be small therapeutic communities, with special methods in each; 3. Results should be tested by comparing actual recidivism with that predicted on the basis of experience, the base expectancy score."

Certainly there are no such "small therapeutic communities" in California now; instead there are eight overcrowded prisons, with a record high population of almost 25,000, and the gloomy prediction is that by 1972 this will have reached 35,000. New institutions are planned or in

189

course of construction—one of them is to be a medical facility for mentally disturbed youths—but by the time they are open they too will be overcrowded. There are too many prisoners to find work for all of them, and the consequent idleness leads to the facilitating of escapes, the smuggling of narcotics, and to fights which too frequently end in murder. All this tends to obscure the fact that actually, if we must have prisons at all, California basically has the best ones possible under present social circumstances.

California has had a parole system since 1893, and a modified indeterminate sentence law since 1917. This is not a true indeterminate sentence, which theoretically would be from no time at all to life for each prisoner; a minimum and maximum time, both in prison and on parole, are set by the legislature for each offense, but within these limits the Adult Authority fixes the term and grants paroles. The Youth Authority, now copied by Massachusetts, Minnesota, Wisconsin, and Texas, was established in 1941 and decides on the disposition of each juvenile offender after he has been studied in a diagnostic clinic. It has been called "the most important advance in correctional thought since the 1870's."

The Institute for Men, at Chino, near Los Angeles, is the largest open (but fence-enclosed) prison in the country and is considered the best of its kind—with Wallkill, New York, and Seagoville, Texas, not far behind. It was the first minimum-security prison in the United States on its precise pattern. Now it has an overflow branch at Tehachapi, formerly the site of the Institution for Women, before an earthquake caused removal of that prison to Corona. At Tehachapi, and to a lesser extent at Chino itself, the prison regimen centers around group activities; there are fifty counseling groups which meet for an hour and a half a week, and two "living groups" which meet for an hour a day. At Pine Hall, Chino's "therapeutic clinic" has men living and working together in an atmosphere which prepares them for life on their discharge. For eight weeks before his release the inmate must attend special pre-release group meetings. Visitors may meet and lunch with inmates out of doors on the 1250-acre plant. But even Chino's model conditions are now being nullified by the omnipresent overcrowding.

The Medical Center at Vacaville (moved to Central California from Terminal Island off San Pedro) is also a model for others of its kind, but it too is understaffed and overpopulated. Sixty to 70 per cent of its cases are psychiatric, and it also accommodates tuberculous patients and others with chronic diseases. In general, medical and surgical care in California prisons is excellent, and as a matter of routine it includes plastic surgery for the disfigured, the removal of stigmatic tattoos, and the repair of dental anomalies. Felons from the forty-seven northern counties of the state's fifty-eight, and all parole violators, may undergo medical study at Vacaville, felons from Southern California at Chino, women at Corona.

Corona, which houses all woman felons, trains its inmates in five vocational fields, including practical nursing and cosmetology, as well as giving academic courses up to junior college. Its fully accredited hospital is now carrying on cancer research with inmate volunteers, in cooperation with the College of Medical Evangelists. At Corona, the women do all the farming and maintenance work as well as household tasks and sewing.

The Youth Authority usually sends its older and more serious cases to Soledad or to the Deuel Vocational Institution in Tracy, both adult institutions, rather than to a reformatory, where it is felt that this affords a better program for rehabilitation. The Reception-Guidance Center at Deuel serves primarily as a diagnostic facility for

191

Youth Authority wards. It receives them directly from the county jails and processes them to Deuel itself or to a Youth Authority Training School. Deuel has a Pilot Intensive Counseling Organization, a joint program in which 125 men live in a house with twelve staff members.

Folsom, orginally a prison for recidivists and still largely in the same category, lags behind the other California prisons in attaining contemporary standards of penology. It has 2891 inmates, with a capacity of 2350, and its physical equipment makes proper classification and treatment difficult. But against these obstacles it is doing the best it can to modernize its system.

Even in Folsom the days of stone-breaking and dungeons are over. Everywhere in the state the dungeon has given way to "adjustment centers" within the institutions—separate cells, with close security and segregation, but with individual treatment and, if possible, occupational therapy. To these centers are consigned not only recalcitrant trouble-makers, but also "blatant homosexuals, the emotionally disturbed, and escape risks." It is, as the Department of Corrections says, "a long, progressive step from the pre-modern 'hole' where balky prisoners were put on bread and water. Penologists long since have discovered that such treatment improved no one, simply made them worse. . . . The effort continues to find some technique, some approach that may spell change in their behavior pattern."

Though the lower ranks of prison personnel still leave much to be desired, the status of employees is constantly improving. There have often been good wardens, but never before so many good guards. All prison employees, including the supervisory staff, undergo continuous in- and out-institution training throughout their incumbency. Since 1954 guards have been trained in group counseling, under the direction of Dr. Norman Fenton, a psychologist. Staff in-service training classes are mandatory, and staff members are also encouraged to do outside study at colleges near the institution where they are employed.

California prisoners no longer wear any sort of humiliating uniforms; the men have blue denim jeans and jackets, with white jackets for hospital workers, the women wear gingham dresses with their own choice of color. Self-respect is fostered by such minor recognition of a prisoner's status as a human being. It is reflected in the growth of participation in such voluntary activities as academic education and contributions to the public good (e.g., blood donations).

In the prison population it was found that, at entrance, 3 per cent of the inmates were illiterate, little more than one-third had ever attended a high school, and only 3 per cent had been graduated from one. In 1959 and 1960, California prisoners were awarded 402 high school diplomas (one to a 50-year-old man) and 801 elementary school diplomas. Five hundred twenty-three inmates completed correspondence school courses, and 1587 earned certificates for completion of courses in art, music, and other special subjects.

There are other supplementary features of California's penal system which are of interest, such as the outside Trade Advisory Committee which since 1942 has trained inmates of nine state institutions for jobs in industry after their release, and which gives advice to the Inmate Vocational Trades Council. Larry Balch, himself an ex-convict, has established a "Halfway House" (along the lines of similar official institutions in England) for newly released men with no homes of their own and is now seeking the approval of the Department of Corrections to be allowed to take in those on parole as well as those discharged. One of the most hopeful plans, previously alluded to, is that instituted by the former sheriff of Santa Clara County, Melvin L. Hawley, under whose jurisdiction selected county prisoners worked outside the jail during the day, paying the county $3.50 a day for room and board. Now the present sheriff, Jack Gibbons, is trying to expand the program in order to permit state prisoners who are Santa Clara County residents to be released a little earlier than the expiration of their sentences and sent home to be put under this same system and thus "be given a tempering process between the rigidity of imprisonment and the freedom of ordinary society." He hopes that this will reduce the rate of recidivism, since it has been demonstrated that the rate of return to crime is highest during the six months after a man leaves prison.

San Quentin, oldest and largest of California's prisons, deserves particular mention, especially since the malodorous actions of a small minority of its inmates have recently given the prison a bad name it has not earned.

As has been said, sporadic outbursts such as the escapes and murders early in 1962 are a result of congestion and of consequent idleness. San Quentin is, next to the Michigan State Penitentiary at Jackson, the largest prison in the United States. As Warden Richard Dickson says, it is "an industrial prison with 4000 men assigned to full-time jobs; . . . this is to keep the men busy. The problem we always have is with the 1000 who are not assigned, the idle. Besides, many prisoners are sent to San Quentin from other institutions where they were trouble-makers. We are going to sift them and either send them elsewhere or segregate them."

Administrator of Corrections McGee says that the state will "make an immediate search for a facility capable of handling 1000 or more from San Quentin. We're always behind in construction." Governor Edmund G. Brown has announced a budget of $72 million for prison facilities for 1962–63, $10 million more than in the preceding fiscal year, but even so the rising crime rate, especially among the young, is crowding all the prisons to the gunwales. The new medium-security Men's Colony East, at San Luis Obispo, adjacent to the California Men's Colony (which is for older men only), has 1400 inmates even though it is not yet finished. Some of the young prisoners in Deuel and Soledad will be sent to reformatories to make room for more of San Quentin's surplus. Others may be moved to the former Mojave Marine Base, now the property of Kern County. One of the best features of California's system, the sending of older reliable men into forest camps, unfortunately leaves a concentration of tough young prisoners behind.

So much for San Quentin's present troubles. There remains one of the best and best-run prisons in the world.

We have caught, from time to time, in other connections, glimpses of the hell-hole which San Quentin once was, from the days when it began in a prison hulk because the nearest penitentiary to California was six hundred miles away. We have seen barefoot, filthy prisoners (one bath a week, the same cold water plunge used by all, diseased or not) working in chains under fear of the lash. We have seen Negro prisoners, in the early days, sent to New Orleans and sold into slavery. We have seen the dungeons where men were chained to an iron eye embedded in the stone wall. Against Governor Brown's budget of $72 million, let us put the year 1867, when it cost just $63.80 to keep a prisoner alive for a year! In 1881, the lieutenant governor announced smugly: "The cruel and inhuman rule usual at prisons is not in vogue here. Instead, we treat all who will bear it with kindness and even courtesy." Then he ordered extra wages for a guard to act as official flogger.

Kenneth Lamott has told the whole sorry story of the

prison in its early days in his *Chronicles of San Quentin*. But he has also marked the gradual improvements, sometimes abortive, but permanent cumulatively.

John E. Hoyle, who took office in 1907, was San Quentin's first reform warden, with real principles and a real program. There had been others in the past who meant well, and there were others after him. James A. Johnston, who had been warden at Folsom and was later to be warden at Alcatraz, was one of the good ones (Though he eschewed such sentimental gestures as Hoyle's Christmas stockings and Easter eggs and female prisoners sent out once a month to pick wild flowers!). When he resigned in 1924, Lamott notes, a newspaper said that "San Quentin today is a sort of university and health center combined." (It was not, and it is not now: no prison is or can be.)

In 1940, it was Clinton T. Duffy who finally headed the prison in the direction of an enlightened modern penal institution. Duffy's monumental work is too well known to make it necessary to go into detail about it. But it must be remembered that he would have failed, as so many progressive men failed before him, if it had not been for the establishment of the new Department of Corrections in 1944. Duffy, for extraneous reasons, had himself opposed the prison reorganization bill which created the department; nevertheless, it was this radical reorganization which made possible the progress since passage of the bill.

A particular account of the rehabilitative organizations and activities at San Quentin today would be merely a duplication of what has been said already of other modern prisons. Like any institution, it has its own individual features and is often in the news for good as well as bad reasons. (At the same time as the sensational stories of stabbings and dope smuggling, it was noted in California papers that every prisoner under forty at San Quentin was to be given a chance for polio shots. It has also just been revealed that for the first time in the prison's history, inmates are being taken outside under guard to participate in a medical research program; ten selected volunteers are acting as guinea pigs in a study of breathing and blood physiology at Mount Zion Hospital in San Francisco.) Recently at a "press day" in the prison, when outside newspaper men helped the inmate staff to get out an edition of the prison's biweekly paper, a reporter asked nine inmates at random, "What rules would you like to see changed?" Many of the answers were trivial, but some were revealing. "It is obsolete to have guns all around; it makes a person feel like an animal." "There should be new facilities to handle more visitors; I have only half an hour a month with my wife." "The wording of the rules pertaining to the conduct of officers and inmates is too general and not clear; it should be changed." Can one imagine a San Quentin prisoner of 1862 daring to voice such criticisms? Another symptomatic note is the number of voluntary Sunday lock-ups, with unlocks for meals, movies, and visits to the canteen. Once Sunday lock-up was a form of punishment, with no meals served, but now men with study or handicrafts to get on with prefer a day alone in their cells, built for one, in which they can find privacy. A producer who made a movie in San Quentin, wrote to the warden after his first experience "inside": "My only problem was that I constantly forgot where I was. . . . The 'climate' in your prison lays so much emphasis on giving an inmate a chance to find the right road back to society, that in an entire week of shooting I never experienced a single tremor of fear."

Despite its problems, San Quentin is a good example of the motto of the Department of Corrections: "Good custody is good treatment, and good treatment is good custody." It has played a prominent part in the California Conservation Plan, which through forestry camps and fire fighting units makes "a joint effort to save the State's natural resources, and its human resources, too." It is deeply involved in ICE, the plan's program of Increased Correctional Effectiveness, which through therapeutic community living, intensive parole supervision, and group counseling endeavors to "tie together the results of years of experiment and research into a rehabilitational package."

9

By and large, then, California stands as an outstanding example of the best that a state penal system can offer today. What of the Federal prison system? Though in some respects England equals or outdoes it, it too has grown into an organization among the very best of its kind. (It was not in a Federal prison, but in a Marine barracks on Okinawa, that a man not yet tried was kept for forty-three days in a five-by-seven-foot concrete "sweatbox," without heat, light, a bed, or hot food.)

The oldest Federal prison is McNeil Island, Washington, opened as a territorial prison in 1867. As late as 1930 there were only five. Atlanta, Georgia, and Leavenworth, Kansas, followed McNeil Island, and then came Alderson, West Virginia, for women, and Chillicothe Reformatory in Ohio. Before them, misdemeanants and even felons were farmed out to county jails and some state prisons; in fact, some still are. There are now six Federal penitentiaries, four reformatories, seven prison camps, and fifteen other institutions of various kinds. Like the state prisons, the Federal institutions are overcrowded—an average of eight hundred to a thousand new prisoners are added every year. The Lompoc, California, institution for young offenders living on the West Coast and the Sandstone, Minnesota, correctional institute for adults from the Middle West were added in 1960, and a new maximum security prison is being constructed at Marion, Illinois. The prison

198

camps, in national forests or on Army reservations, are for "improvable" male misdemeanants, plus a very few "honor men" among the felons who are committed directly to them. Civil misdemeanants go to the reformatory at Petersburg, Virginia, or to other nearer reformatories; a very few are sent to the Medical Center in Springfield, Missouri, and some narcotics addicts are put on probation on condition that they voluntarily enter the hospital in Lexington, Kentucky, or Fort Worth, Texas. There are also Federal institutions in Alaska and Hawaii.

The so-called correctional institutions were formerly known as Federal jails (Alaska's, in Fairbanks and Anchorage, still are). They contain, as the Federal Bureau of Prisons puts it, "the confidence man and the sharecropper, the auto thief, the moonshiner, the forger, the counterfeiter, the hobo, the tax evader, the alcoholic, the embezzler, all thrown together in a strange restricted environment and all wanting one thing above all else—to get out and stay out." These are civilian breakers of Federal laws; military prisoners who have committed felonies go to one of the penitentiaries, and their average term is twelve years as opposed to the civilian average, which ranges from ten months for immigration law offenders to five years and eight months for narcotics offenders. (Usually, however, the actual time served is about half the sentence.)

The prisoner committed to a Federal Correctional Institution spends his first four months in the admission and orientation department, where he is tested and evaluated for classification. There are thirty kinds of work to which he may be assigned, including construction training and office work, but most of the inmates are assigned to farm work, since the institutions are nearly all in agricultural areas. Education is voluntary; if a man signs up for classes he works half a day and goes to school the other half. The educational level of inmates is far below the national average, with 40 per cent having had less than fifth-grade schooling. At the Tallahassee institution, which may be taken as typical, there is a library of 8000 books, there are classes in music appreciation, weekly movies, athletics, occasional debates with outside teams from high schools and colleges, and plays presented by outsiders. There is a full-time Protestant chaplain, who also directs group therapy and gives individual counseling, and Roman Catholic and Jewish chaplains visit regularly. Leave is granted for the funerals of near relatives. In other words, these are thoroughly modern penal institutions.

Lewisburg, Pennsylvania, may be taken as an example of the Federal medium security prison, stricter than the reformatories but less rigorous than, say, Atlanta or Leavenworth. This penitentiary has two honor camps, which raise beef and vegetables for prison use. It has an interesting Social Education program, given through lectures and discussion groups, and other advanced features such as outdoor visiting. The dining room is run cafeteria style with tables for four, and the men, instead of being marched to and from meals, may eat whenever they choose between specified hours.

The blot on the Federal prison system is Alcatraz. This island shaped like a battleship, planted in the middle of San Francisco Bay, greets travelers from the Pacific as the Statue of Liberty greets those from the Atlantic. It was formerly an Army Disciplinary Barracks, where conscientious objectors were lodged during World War I. There is a strong movement to abolish it, especially as it is falling to pieces physically and it would cost $4 million to renovate it. One might wonder if it does not constitute "cruel and unusual punishment" to compel a prisoner, day and night, to see before him the buildings and lights of San Francisco, which it is utterly impossible for him to reach —the undertow in the Bay is so strong that no prisoner has ever been known to escape; five have tried it in two separate escapes up to date, and at this writing all are thought to have been drowned. All supplies, including fresh water, must be brought to the island from the mainland by boat. Upkeep per prisoner is more than $10 a day, while at Atlanta, for example, it is $3. Lieutenant Governor Glenn M. Anderson of California has called Alcatraz "a psychological and aesthetic disgrace."

But "The Rock," as it known, has its stout defenders. Warden Olin Blackwell says it is necessary to deter prisoners in other Federal penitentiaries from becoming trouble-makers: "The fear of being sent to Alcatraz keeps them in line." However, if such a super-maximum security prison, out of step with everything in modern penology, is really needed, there is no reason why it should not be established elsewhere. Then, as architect Allan Temko suggests, the island might be developed as a public park, where the underground dungeons at least might be preserved as a historical monument. "Children could be shown where human beings were kept in solitary confinement, and if they take fright, could be reassured . . . that this had occurred long ago, and like goblins and ogres had vanished from the civilized earth."

Although this recommendation has not been carried out (nor is it likely to be in the near future), the Federal Bureau of Prisons does do all it can to bring Alcatraz into conformity with modern prison practice. It was, the Bureau says, established "for those who do not readily accustom themselves to the discipline of the ordinary penitentiary or avail themselves of the opportunities for training and self-improvement. . . . They are all men guilty of serious crimes, who make difficult the maintenance of discipline and retard the efforts to rehabilitate the greater percentage of our prison population." The authorities insist that commitment to Alcatraz is a matter of discipline and is not intended "to make punishment more severe." The inmates do not agree. Alcatraz has a bad record of riot and mutiny. The worst were the "blast out" attempts in 1939 and 1946, in the latter of which two officers and three prisoners were killed. But the administration says the prisoners have "earned their way into Alcatraz and can and do earn their way out." They point out that no single inmate who was committed there when "the Rock" became a prison for civilians in 1934 is still a prisoner there.

There are shops in which the men receive "modest wages," and no prisoner is forced to work in them, though he must do some kind of work if he is physically able. Shop workers may also earn some reduction of their sentence—though this cannot be much of an incentive to the 19 men with life sentences and the 15 more with terms of from 45 to 199 years! There is no actual school, but the men can take correspondence courses in the University of California, San Francisco State College, and the International Correspondence School. They are not allowed to have daily papers, but there is a library of 15,000 books. There is no commissary or canteen, but there are biweekly movies, and 20 per cent of the inmates do some kind of art work. They have two hours of radio at night, are allowed two packs of cigarettes a week, may write two letters a week and receive one a day, and can have authorized visitors once a month.

The men are locked up fourteen hours a day, from five p.m. on, with fourteen head counts during the twenty-four hours, and constant shakedowns. The cells, for single occupancy, are five by nine feet, containing a wall bunk, a table, a toilet, and a wash basin. In D block, the "treatment unit" for rule-breakers, they sleep on mattresses on the floor, have a reduced diet, sometimes are forbidden a light, and are allowed out only for exercise in the yard. There is one guard for every two and a half prisoners, as against one for ten in the other penitentiaries, and though the guards in the corridors are unarmed, armed guards cover them from above.

The controversial question of Alcatraz aside, Federal prisons do operate on the principle that "men are committed to prison as, not for, punishment . . . Obviously, if the prison life only makes [a man] more vindictive and sullen, or furthers his education in crime, the lives and property of people will later be placed in jeopardy."

All Federal prison personnel is under Civil Service. The fourteen hospitals are all accredited. There is a cancer detection clinic at the Alderson Reformatory for Women, and other prisons have carried on research, with prisoner volunteers, in malaria, polio, the common cold, and other disorders. Up to 13,000 prisoners have made blood donations to the Red Cross. Psychiatrists are being trained at the Menninger Clinic in Topeka, Kansas, and are being added as fast as possible. With 20–25 per cent of newly committed Federal prisoners totally illiterate, some 2400 underwent literacy training in 1960. Eight thousand more took at least one high school course, and in some cases they received diplomas from the state in which the prison is located. About half of the 5000 or more assigned to vocational courses finished them. A placement unit found jobs for 1735 men on their release, with 205 of these jobs directly related to the vocational training they received in prison.

One very interesting development is Federal Prison Industries, Inc., which exists to expand the opportunities for job experience for prisoners. In 1960 it opened five new industrial operations in various institutions—electronics, furniture refinishing, a canvas specialty shop, equipment repair, and manufacture of rubber products—bringing the total to date to forty-nine shops and factories. Both government and civilian teachers are employed, and the industry is kept on a level with that in the outside world.

In 1960, administrative personnel from the state prisons of Montana and Utah were given a week of intensive training at McNeil Island, to enable them to train their own staffs. Kansas, Missouri, and Oklahoma have also benefited from this type of training by Federal inspectors.

The incidence of young offenders in Federal institutions has increased 137 per cent since 1937. This enormous increase constitutes a problem. A new law extends the Youth Corrections Act to persons between twenty-two and twenty-five, who, under alternative sentencing procedures, may be committed to the custody of the Attorney General for a period of study, diagnosis, and recommendations. Minors are not included under this provision, though in fact they have been admitted to it. But they can no longer be transferred elsewhere from the National Training School in Washington, D.C., though many of them are "physically mature and quite sophisticated in their delinquent behavior."

These and other problems are under consideration in the Bureau's close liaison with the research program of the University of Illinois on recidivism, a four-year project which will be completed by 1963. The Bureau has also started a new research project of its own, covering "certain segments of specific programs." With an all-time-high prison population of 24,084 (not counting military or naval prisoners) in 1959–60, 4 per cent higher than the year before, and a specially marked increase in drug-law violators, study of this sort becomes increasingly urgent.

Summing up its basic philosophy, the Federal Bureau of Prisons says it is fundamentally "implementation of an individualized system of discipline, care, and treatment." But, it adds, "the decade ahead may become a period of re-evaluation of many of the more traditional correctional methods and greater experimentation with newer techniques." We may expect a closer integration of the judicial and sentencing process with the program of institutions, and "greater reliance on community resources for the eventual rehabilitation of the offender."

With this forecast we leave today's prison and begin to extrapolate from penological history the probable shape of the prison of tomorrow.

Section 3

TOMORROW'S PRISONS

1

What will the prisons of the future be like? Shall we recognize them as prisons at all, by today's standards? As we have seen, the history of prisons as places of punishment for specific crimes (as opposed to places of detention until other punishment is rendered) is not very long. What we take for granted now may be merely a transient phenomenon.

There is no immediate prospect of any decline in the rapidly growing crime rate. Crimes against persons and property—the basic foundations of criminality, so to speak —will continue and almost certainly increase, and new offenses are constantly being created by the passage of new laws making illegal what has hitherto been legal. (An example of this action is the sale of alcoholic liquor during the Prohibition era.) Dr. Joseph D. Lohman, Dean of Criminology at the University of California, has put this prospect in very cogent terms. He figures that at the current rate of population growth, the United States will have 200 million inhabitants by 1970 and perhaps more than 300 million by the end of the century. As a joint consequence of the prolongation of life and the unchecked birth rate, there will concomitantly be a growth in disproportion in the population, with the very young and the very old constituting continually rising percentages of the whole. As he puts it, by 1970 there will be "100 mouths, or unproductive people, for 100 hands, or the productive age group."

It is the young particularly, further influenced by the concentration of people in the metropolitan areas, who furnish and will continue to furnish the rising figures in crime. In 1957, most convicted criminals were in their twenties; today, over 60 per cent of serious crime is committed by those under eighteen. On the basis of these statistics, Dr. Lohman predicts a 44 per cent increase in crime in the next decade.

If this be true, the question of what to do with all these new criminals—to say nothing of the old habituals and professionals who will still be with us—becomes a terribly urgent one. Short of having our whole civilization and most of our population wiped out by a fission bomb, we are going to keep on having laws, with more and more people breaking them, and the penologists will have to find the answer, if one is to be found.

To meet this challenge adequately, we shall have to change a good many firmly grounded concepts, and in many ways start all over again. The difficulty is that most of the public (i.e., the people who furnish the funds, through taxes), when they are not hysterically protesting "coddling," are completely apathetic. Hugh Klare, secretary of the Howard League for Prison Reform, put this in a nutshell when he said: "Just because there have been great improvements in penal methods, and the evils of the present system are much less serious, . . . public apathy and complacency are perhaps harder to control than ever."

Hermann Mannheim has called the belief in punishment as deterrence the greatest single obstacle in the development of efficient methods of penology; he considers it completely incompatible with real reformation. It may be doubted whether one murderer ever stayed his hand, or one burglar kept away from an inviting haul, simply because he knew that if he was caught he would go to prison or worse. Others may get into trouble, but we ourselves are always safe whatever risks we take—which within limits is more or less plausible. It is true that for the most part the criminals who are caught and convicted are the stupid, the inept, or the unlucky.

Yet there is no denying that revenge and retribution, with deterrence as their excuse, are the guiding principles of the uninformed. The average law-abiding taxpayer is much more likely to want to "get even" with the law-breaker (unless one should turn up in his own family or among his own friends) than he is to desire his rehabilitation and to be willing to pay what it costs to rehabilitate him through individual therapy.

The economic motif, therefore, is still strong. Since, as Klare says, "No one has yet succeeded in providing a full day's work of a reasonably constructive kind" for all prisoners, there is no chance of their being self-supporting and still less of their being a profitable asset to the state. As a result, Bentham's Principle of Less Eligibility still obtains—the condition of the criminal, his food, clothing, and way of living, should be at the very least not higher than that of the poorest noncriminal. Even reform schools for the young still, according to Louis Robinson, "retain the older notion that the standard of living within the prison must be below the minimum standard outside." And he adds that times of economic crisis always lead to intensification of this principle, which in the long run is itself an economic waste: the worse the conditions, the less likely a prisoner is to strive for his own reformation. The living conditions of any prison are, of course, hardest on those who are used to better things, but the poorest pris-

209

oner can be made insubordinate and resentful when he finds things even worse in prison than they were for him outside.

That is only one small facet of the problem confronting the penologist today. The advocates of the "treat 'em rough" school are still vocal, and many of them are in places of power. "Aside from his rehabilitation," which he granted had occurred, "we say he has not served enough time to fit the crime," said the District Attorney of Philadelphia recently in discussing a murderer's plea for parole. When England currently debated the question of restoring flogging in prisons, Robert Fabian, the noted former Detective Superintendent of New Scotland Yard, told the *London Observer* that he favored it, and Professor Leon Radzinowics, the retiring president of the British Academy of Forensic Sciences, agreed that 65 per cent of the general public would be for it, "as some extra quality in the field of deterrents." A prominent San Francisco attorney jeers at "an attitude which is unfortunately widespread, that punishment is intended solely to rehabilitate the individual offender." As for J. Edgar Hoover, head of the FBI, he is notoriously one of the "hard boiled" school. "I am disgusted," he exploded, "by misguided sentimentalists who want to pamper and excuse teen-age thugs." Whenever a man uses such words as "pamper" and "coddle" in regard to modern penology, you may take it for granted that he has very little real idea of what it is all about. To Hoover, all criminals are merely "mad dogs" who should be exterminated, and all prison reformers are "moo-cow sentimentalists."

The essence of imprisonment is its deprivation of liberty, and no enlightened penologist has ever suggested that those who deliberately break the law should not be segregated from the free society whose rules they have violated. The question is: Shall such a man be segregated in revenge, made to suffer as a punishment, or should he be kept separate and studied and treated until he can be trusted to be no longer a criminal (which may, in some cases, be never)? Is the prison as it exists today, or in any form in which it could exist and still be a prison, capable of becoming such a place? As David Lamson said in *We Who Are About to Die,* we must decide whether the purpose is to punish offenders or to rehabilitate them. "The two are mutually exclusive. . . . The prison represents a compromise, . . . and hence is ineffective in either direction."

More than a century ago Richard Carlile, who was four times a prisoner though never a criminal, said truly: "I do not believe there ever was an individual possessed of sufficient fortitude to bear a long imprisonment with patience. The prisoner from the moment he enters his dungeon seems to have severed the last link connecting him with human nature." The Federal Bureau of Prisons quotes an inmate of Alcatraz who wrote: "No one knows what it is like to suffer from the intellectual atrophy, the pernicious mental scurvy that comes of long privation of all the things that make life real." (As Leo Rosten remarked, a prison is "the most secure place in the world; you get . . . all the security anybody would want. But nobody wants it.")

An ex-convict named Hal Hollister, writing in *The Saturday Evening Post,* says flatly that "just about every aspect of prison society militates against reform. . . . Reformation in the sense of a moral reawakening is rare in prison." Yet "reformation in the sense of a moral reawakening" is precisely the end in view of modern penology. If Hollister is right, can prisons be so altered as to bring about that end, or must some other form of treatment of criminality be devised?

J. J. Cacopardo, a reformed criminal who is now a cler-

211

gyman, would say that no prison, however enlightened, can free itself of Lamson's "compromise." "If the prisoner has a few humanitarian comforts such as good food, movies, a radio, as he may well have in the Federal prisons and more 'enlightened' state prisons," he says in his *Show Me a Miracle*, "these tantalizing privileges only serve as painful reminders of all the other things he once took for granted which are now denied him." To him the best prison presents only "the stresses and strains of an unnatural life of caged loneliness without privacy." Granted that to less articulate and impressionable men Cacopardo's torment would seem grossly exaggerated, nevertheless he represents exactly the sort of offender who is susceptible to reformation, and if the prison fails with such men (it was through other influences that he himself was rehabilitated) then some other way must be discovered to do the work of reform. As C. Fletcher-Cooke, of the British Home Office, wrote in the *Manchester Guardian,* "imprisonment is a negative form of treatment, and experience shows that such methods are rarely successful."

There are, indeed, many penologists who do believe that the prison can be altered and adapted to make it a rehabilitative force, without its being abolished and by substituting for it some other way to deal with crime. Bernard Shaw's "crime of imprisonment" is to them, so to speak, a misdemeanor rather than a felony. *Mere* imprisonment without treatment is, as Royce Brier remarked in the *San Francisco Chronicle,* "a slovenly makeshift for which society itself is initially responsible." The Federal Bureau of Prisons thinks "prisons . . . are merely vast human warehouses, degrading and self-defeating, . . . or dynamic instrumentalities for the reshaping of character"; and it has no doubt that they can be made into the latter image. Sybille Bedford, in *The Faces of Punishment,* has set the problem squarely before us: "We are becoming more and

212

more uneasy about prisons. Should penalties be mainly deterrents? Do deterrents deter? . . . Many people would no longer say they were *for* prison; they might say, but how could we do without, what should we do? Sentencing, sending a man to prison, is a fearful thing; [but] then so are many forms of crime."

There are many suggestions for reformation of the prison system. One is a true indeterminate sentence, not the approximation to it we have now: a sentence that would not merely pronounce minimum and maximum terms, but would provide for individual treatment until the subject is cured of his criminal bent, whether that be soon, a long time, or never—just as is the case in good mental hospitals today, whereas once a psychotic's stay in an "asylum" was determined by anything but scientific considerations.

Another dilemma is that of uniform treatment of all convicted of specific crimes, as against specialized institutions based on the nature of the offender, not of the offense. One aspect of this is that fearful problem, the young criminal who is yet not a juvenile delinquent: should such offenders, between, say, eighteen and twenty-five, be sent to the same institutions and receive the same treatment as those in older age groups? (This is very different from J. Edgar Hoover's recommendation that all youths and boys, however young, who commit crimes of violence should be relegated to ordinary felony prisons.) Barnes and Teeters say not; they feel that youths in this age group "present very definite personality and adjustment problems that require specialized understanding, consideration, and treatment not to be found in 'good' prisons for adults."

Clinton Duffy advocates "minimum security institutions for all but the worst trouble-makers who need the most intensive therapy." Walter Dunbar, California's Director of Corrections, wants "half-way houses, parolee work camps and advisory groups, short-term confinement centers, and community correctional centers."

The Federal Bureau of Prisons, which believes existing prisons can be made adequate to deal with these and all other problems, nevertheless perceives the reality and strength of the challenge. "What will the prison of tomorrow be like?" it asks. "Penology is yet in its infancy as a science, and treatment is the newest of its concepts. . . . Research into the effectiveness of prison programs appears to be the next giant step forward toward our goal of a greater percentage of restored, successful citizens."

Some of this research has already been undertaken. C. H. Rolph, who is a former chief police inspector and is now on the executive committee of the Howard League, in an open letter to the British Home Secretary which was printed in the *New Statesman & Nation,* offered a series of recommendations that he felt would transform prisons into true centers of rehabilitation. They must, he said, be drastically changed, cut into smaller units, with no more than 150 prisoners in each; "in fact, the prison system of the future should be an improvement on the Borstal system of today." The present buildings, he said, were "too vast and too old." (And yet how much less vast and often how much less old than American penitentiaries!) Prison labor must be "purposeful and of value to the community," and must be paid for at the going rate, with the prisoners saving enough of their pay to support themselves for at least the first two weeks after release and to contribute to the livelihood of their families. There must be adequate after-care. Prison staffs must become trained professional case workers, who would be able to guide group therapy and to preside over consultative meetings between inmates and staff members. Above all—and here he is overwhelmingly right—there must be an inten-

214

sive campaign of public education to rouse citizens from their apathy and to explain to them the reasons for the stated aims of today's penologists.

Louis W. Robinson also believes that the prison system needs reform rather than revolution. He advocates an extension of probation, provision for paying fines by installments, special institutions for scientifically classified types of offenders, and the elimination of all county and city jails as places of incarceration of convicted offenders. All prisons of whatever sort, he says, should be under the jurisdiction of the State Department of Education. (There have been some strange jurisdictions over prison systems: in British India prisons were controlled by the medical branch of the civil administration, and we have noted that until recently all North Carolina's prisons came under the Department of Highways.)

"Let us cease," Robinson says, "to store the criminal away for a few years to deteriorate, and then hand him back to the world. . . . Rather, let us have factory plants to which our criminals shall come as the raw material—some of it rather damaged, to be sure. An institution can certainly alter men's physiques if it goes about it as definitely as a factory would treat silk or steel. Wise, consecrated endeavor will find a way to alter their minds and habits, too."

But could such an institution be called or thought of as a prison, as the word is understood today? And as to the more detailed recommendations, how do they differ from what the more advanced penal institutions are already doing?

There are other penologists and criminologists who would abandon the entire prison concept, and put in its place a system which approximates medical treatment of the physically and mentally ill. To quote Richard Drinnon, in *Rebel in Paradise*, they feel that "the prison is simply an anachronism which perpetuates and multiplies crime, . . . that such a malignant tumor requires a major operation, not placebos, that . . . prisons should be torn down, not patched up."

They know that opposed to them will be all who believe in freedom of the will and who consider criminality not a disease but a deliberate choosing of evil. But, as Tolbert McCarroll says, "every individual who degrades others degrades himself, and our penal system degrades all society." And Robinson himself adds: "The penal system of any given society is not an isolated phenomenon subject only to its own special laws. It is an integral part of the whole social system and shares its aspirations and defects." It is, as Barnes and Teeters call it, a sociomedical problem. Proof is overwhelming that cruelty and severe repression, and what Kenneth Lamott calls "the curious combination of guilt, vengefulness, and prurient fascination that has been the dominant theme in the treatment of our criminals," have failed utterly to end or even to lessen crime.

What specifically would take the place of our present jails and prisons if they were abolished, is for penology to determine. Dr. Karl A. Menninger gives a hint of the probable trend. In an article in *Harper's* Magazine he forecasts "a diversified institutional system and treatment program," with the former jails serving as "diagnostic clearing houses or classification units," and wide use of an authentic indeterminate sentence, since diagnosis and rehabilitation may require any variety of security measures, from minimum to maximum. Then, "if the prisoner cannot be changed by genuine efforts to rehabilitate him, we must look *our* failures in the face" and provide for his indefinitely continued detention.

The "new prison," Barnes and Teeters assert, is no solution whatever of the problems surrounding "the stupid benighted treatment of some 200,000 inmates languishing in our correctional institutions and another million or more cooped up in county jails, most of which are not fit for human habitation." "The fundamental truth," they add, is that "we shall not make any substantial progress merely by advocating better correctional institutions. There must be a complete escape from all institutionalization, save for the few who need permanent segregation or a short period of institutional experience before conditional release under supervision." What they foresee ultimately is "the replacement of prisons by a flexible program of reformative treatment based on reason and science." This of course will imply parole officers in numbers far in excess of all prison staffs today.

It will not be easy, and it will not come soon. There are some who are pessimistic about its ever coming at all —men such as M. Hamblin Smith, who says that penal problems "have been solved and will continue to be solved not in conformity with criminological and penological factors, but according to economic expediency."

But even economic expediency is to some extent on the side of the reformers, if the public can be educated to realize that their program will in the long run be economically as well as socially beneficial. A man earning his own living and supporting his family, both during and after his "treatment," is surely more of a saving to the taxpayer than one who has to be supported at great expense and whose family has to go on public relief (to say nothing of the tremendous property losses caused by the unredeemed burglar or embezzler!). If not for the sake of the deviant human being, then perhaps for the sake of his own pocketbook, the man in the street may some day be persuaded to give the penologists a chance to try their way.

That chance is our only hope of lessening the huge

burden of crime that lies heavy on the shoulders of every civilized nation. For, as Ruggles-Brise remarks, "Deprivation of liberty is, after all the only and the greatest punishment," and a man is just as much deprived of liberty in a quasi-hospital-cum-school as he is in a prison. So, says Ruggles-Brise, "After 2000 years we are coming back to the old Roman definition of prison," as a place for detaining people, not a place for punishing them.

If we do not return to this concept—which implies the disappearance of prisons in the sense in which we now understand the word, whatever the "treatment institutions" may be called—then we might as well reconcile ourselves to the idea that we shall always have criminals and shall never be able to rehabilitate all or most of them. Kenneth Lamott has put our dilemma into succinct words: "Nobody has ever presented any convincing proof that the modern prison has rehabilitated a larger proportion of its inmates than the tough prison of the last century. . . . Decency and common sense, a little psychiatry and a little religion have proved to be not enough. . . . If we can ever summon up the courage to admit the bankruptcy that hides behind the fine, self-deceiving words, perhaps things will be better some time in the future. [Warden] Harley Teets once said that San Quentin was a blindfolded elephant lumbering along the edge of a precipice. Unhappily, this will probably continue to be the best description of any American [or other] prison that has ever been made."

And "Flag" (Francis Lagrange), the artist-counterfeiter from French Guiana, utters the same warning from the other side of the bars: "It is absurd to pretend indignation at the abuses of an entire system that is itself an abuse. . . . Our penal institutions are the logical result of our concept of justice by punishment: in creating the prison, society does not so much protect [itself from] as revenge itself upon the criminal."

Men and women who commit crimes, even serious crimes, and even men and women who have made a profession of crime, are still human beings, subject to all the improvement and all the deterioration to which every other human being, under the stress of circumstance, is subject. They can be made into wild animals or worse, but so can you and I. They are hardly likely to be transformed into angels, but neither are you and I. Even the worst young hoodlum was once a malleable baby, and unless he is a congenital psychopath (in which case he is a subject for a psychiatrist) he can under proper treatment be reconverted into a normal social being. But it is very improbable that simply committing him to any existing penal institution, however advanced and enlightened, will bring about that transformation.

Penologists are well aware of this. In the words of Max Grünhut, "The outstanding feature of the present movement is its skepticism concerning imprisonment altogether, and its search for new and more adequate methods of treatment outside prison walls."

In a word, the great movement for prison reform, whose often discouraging and yet hopeful history we have surveyed, must in the end, for its real success, be self-liquidating. Its final mission is to bring about the disappearance of prisons.

BIBLIOGRAPHY

The bibliography of penology is immense. In English alone, I have consulted nearly a hundred books, besides innumerable magazine articles, United Nations publications, governmental reports, yearbooks, etc. Much of the available material, however, is highly technical, and some of it, in view of later developments, is outdated. But here is a brief list of books (not all of them valid today) for the lay reader who is curious to know more about the subject than it has been possible to give in the compass of this book. There is also an enormous number of autobiographical accounts by prisoners and ex-prisoners—many of them politicals—in many countries. I have included three such accounts which deal directly with prison conditions. And John Howard's massive pioneer volume is still in print.

BARNES, HARRY ELMER. *The Story of Punishment*. Boston: The Stratford Company, 1930.

BARNES, HARRY ELMER, AND TEETERS, NEGLEY K. *New Horizons in Criminology* (Book 2, "Penal and Correctional Procedures"). New York: Prentice-Hall, Inc., 1943 (Fourth Edition, 1959). [The best up-to-date authority]

BATES, SANFORD. *Prisons and Beyond*. New York: The Macmillan Company, 1936.

BATESON, CHARLES. *The Convict Ships, 1787–1868*. Glasgow: Brown, Son & Ferguson, Ltd., 1959.

BELLI, MELVIN M. *Belli Looks at Life and Law in Japan.* Indianapolis: Bobbs-Merrill Co., Inc., 1960.

BRANCH-JOHNSON, W. *The English Prison Hulks.* London: Christopher Johnson Publishers Ltd., 1917.

CACOPARDO, J. J. (with Don Weldon). *Show Me a Miracle.* New York: E. P. Dutton & Co., 1961. [A prisoner's-eye view].

CALCOTT, MARY STEVENSON. *Russian Justice.* London: The Macmillan Company, 1935.

Chronicles of Newgate. New York: G. P. Putnam's Sons (Capricorn Books), 1961. [New edition of a classic.]

DUFFY, CLINTON T. *The San Quentin Story.* New York: Doubleday & Co., Inc., 1950.

ERICKSON, GLADYS J. *Warden Ragen of Joliet.* New York: E. P. Dutton & Co., 1957.

FOX, SIR LIONEL W. *The English Prison and Borstal Systems.* London: Routledge & Kegan Paul Ltd., 1952.

FUNCK-BRENTANO, FRANZ. *Legendes et Archives de la Bastille.* Paris: Libraire Hachette, 1909.

GIBSON, EDGAR S. *John Howard.* London: Methuen & Co. Ltd., 1901. [I have found no recent life of Howard.]

GILLIN, JOHN L. *Taming the Criminal.* New York: The Macmillan Company, 1931.

GRÜNHUT, MAX. *Penal Reform.* New York: The Clarendon Press, 1948.

HAMBLIN-SMITH, M. *Prisons and Changing Civilization.* London: John Lane, 1934.

HAYNES, FRED E. *The American Prison System.* New York: McGraw-Hill Book Co., Inc., 1939.

HOBHOUSE, STEPHEN, AND BROCKWAY, A. FENNER (eds.). *English Prisons Today.* London: Longmans, Green & Co., 1922.

HOWARD, D. L. *The English Prisons.* London: Christopher Johnson Publishers Ltd., 1958.

JOHNSTON, JAMES A. *Prison Life Is Different.* Boston: Houghton Mifflin Co., 1937.

KIRCHHEIMER, OTTO, AND RUSCHE, GEORG. *Punishment and Social Structure.* New York: Columbia University Press, 1939.

KOERBER, HELENE. *Soviet Russia Fights Crime*. London: G. Routledge & Sons Ltd., 1934.

LAGRANGE, FRANCIS (with William Murray). *Flag on Devil's Island*. New York: Doubleday & Co., Inc., 1961. [A French ex-convict]

LAMOTT, KENNETH. *Chronicles of San Quentin*. New York: David McKay Co., Inc., 1961.

LAWES, LEWIS E. *Life and Death in Sing Sing*. New York: Doubleday & Co., Inc., 1928.

MANNHEIM, HERMANN. *The Dilemma of Penal Reform*. London: George Allen and Unwin, Ltd., 1957.

MARTIN, JOHN BARTLOW. *Break Down the Walls*. New York: Ballantine Books, Inc., 1954.

MUELLER, GERHARD O. W. *Essays in Criminal Science*. London: Sweet and Maxwell Ltd., 1961.

O'BRIEN, ERIS M. *The Foundation of Australia*. London: Sheed & Ward Ltd., 1937.

OSBORNE, THOMAS MOTT. *Society and Prisons*. New Haven: Yale University Press, 1916.

ROBINSON, LOUIS W. *Penology in the United States*. Philadelphia: John C. Winston Company, 1921.

—— *Treatment of Misdemeanant Prisoners in the United States*. Philadelphia: John C. Winston Company, 1944.

ROLPH, C. H. *Common Sense about Crime and Punishment*. New York: The Macmillan Company, 1961.

ROSE, GORDON. *The Struggle for Penal Reform*. Chicago: Quadrangle Books, Inc., 1961.

RUGGLES-BRISE, SIR EVELYN. *The English Prison System*. London: Macmillan and Company, 1922.

SCUDDER, KENYON. *Prisoners Are People*. New York: Doubleday & Co., Inc., 1952.

SELLIN, THORSTEN. *Pioneering in Penology*. Philadelphia: University of Pennsylvania Press, 1934.

SELLIN, THORSTEN, AND LAMBERT, RICHARD D. (eds.). "Prisons in Transformation," *Annals of the American Academy of Political and Social Science* (Volume 283). Philadelphia: May, 1954.

TASKER, ROBERT JOYCE. *Grimhaven*. New York. Alfred A. Knopf, Inc., 1928. [San Quentin as an inmate saw it]

TEETERS, NEGLEY K. *They Were in Prison*. Philadelphia: John C. Winston Company, 1937.

—— *Penology from Panama to Cape Horn*. Philadelphia: University of Pennsylvania Press (for Temple University), 1946.

TEETERS, NEGLEY K., AND SHEARER, JOHN D. *The Prison at Philadelphia, Cherry Hill*. New York: Columbia University Press, 1957.

TOPPING, C. W. *Canadian Penal Institutions*. Chicago: University of Chicago Press, 1930.

VONHENTIG, HANS. *Punishment*. Edinburgh: William Hodge and Company Limited, 1937.

WATSON, JOHN A. F. *Meet the Prisoner*. London: Jonathan Cape Limited, 1959.

WHITNEY, JANET. *Elizabeth Fry, Quaker Heroine*. Boston: Little, Brown & Co., 1936.

WINES, FREDERICK HOWARD. *Punishment and Reform*. New York: Thomas Y. Crowell Company, 1919.

ZALITCH, JUDAH. *Soviet Administration of the Criminal Law*. Philadelphia: University of Pennsylvania Press, 1931.

INDEX

225

233

234

MIRIAM ALLEN deFORD

Mystery stories, true crime articles, science fiction, poems, labor reports, Latin translations—all have poured in profusion from the pen of Miriam Allen deFord. Born in Philadelphia, she attended Wellesley College, Temple University, and the University of Pennsylvania, and has lived in Boston, Baltimore, and for many years in San Francisco. Her writing career has been long and varied—from public relations work to house organs, and as staff correspondent for a news syndicate. She is at present a member of the Board of the Mystery Writers of America, and is an assistant editor of *The Humanist*. She received the Edgar Allan Poe Award from the Mystery Writers of America, Inc., for *The Overbury Affair* (Chilton), which was voted the best nonfiction crime book for 1960. Other books have been: *Love Children; Who Was When?; They Were San Franciscans; Shaken with the Wind; Psychologist Unretired; Up-Hill All the Way;* and *Penultimates,* a volume of poems. In addition, she has contributed to many anthologies and literary biographical dictionaries. In private life, Miriam Allen deFord is the widow of Maynard Shipley, science writer and historian of capital punishment.

DATE DUE